Solution Focuse
in Alternative Schools

Solution Focused Brief Therapy in Alternative Schools (SFBT) provides a step-by-step guide for how school social workers and counselors can work with other school professionals to create an effective solution focused dropout prevention program. Along with illustrative cases and detailed explanations, the authors detail the curriculum and day-to-day operations of a solution focused dropout prevention program by drawing on the experiences of a school that uses this approach.

Cynthia Franklin, PhD, LCSW, is Associate Dean for Doctoral Education, Stiernberg/Spencer Family Professor in Mental Health at the Steve Hicks School of Social Work at The University of Texas at Austin, and an international expert on solution focused brief therapy.

Calvin L. Streeter, PhD, is Meadows Foundation Centennial Professor in the Quality of Life in the Rural Environment at the Steve Hicks School of Social Work at The University of Texas at Austin, and an expert in community-based practice.

Linda Webb, PhD, is Principal of Gonzalo Garza Independence High School and known internationally for her outstanding contributions to solution focused classrooms and for her leadership in transforming urban schools.

Samantha Guz, MSSW, LSW, is a graduate of the Steve Hicks School of Social Work at The University of Texas at Austin and is a social work practitioner with expertise in at-risk youths in schools.

Solution Focused Brief Therapy in Alternative Schools

Ensuring Student Success and Preventing Dropout

By

**Cynthia Franklin,
Calvin L. Streeter,
Linda Webb, and
Samantha Guz**

Routledge
Taylor & Francis Group
NEW YORK AND LONDON

First published 2018
by Routledge
711 Third Avenue, New York, NY 10017

and by Routledge
2 Park Square, Milton Park, Abingdon, Oxon, OX14 4RN

Routledge is an imprint of the Taylor & Francis Group, an informa business

Library of Congress Cataloging-in-Publication Data
A catalog record for this book has been requested

ISBN: 978-1-138-73591-0 (hbk)
ISBN: 978-1-138-73593-4 (pbk)
ISBN: 978-1-315-18624-5 (ebk)

Typeset in Bembo
by codeMantra

Visit the eResources: www.routledge.com/97811389735934

This book is dedicated to Insoo Kim Berg, MSW, one of the developers of Solution Focused Brief Therapy (SFBT) for her early work in helping us train the teachers and staff at Garza High School. Her vision and inspiration helped us create the solution focused high school. As Insoo affectionately said, "I have adopted and become a parent to a high school." Her commitment, service, and passion for helping students lives on in the lives of many.

Cynthia Franklin

Calvin L. Streeter

Linda Webb

Samantha Guz

Contents

Preface

Imagine working every day in an alternative high school attended by dozens of high-risk adolescents. At any given moment, educators and parents can be challenged by signs of social and emotional crisis, suicide ideation, and challenging behaviors creating stressful interactions and problems in relationships. Alternative high schools frequently serve as dropout prevention programs that educate high-risk adolescents whose academic difficulties and dropout status often coincide with adverse childhood experiences; trauma; behavioral health problems; socioeconomic, family, and cultural stress; and unstable living arrangements. These students are usually labeled "at-risk" by educators who also may view them as sad cases, lost causes, and incorrigible, and as having very limited opportunities to succeed in life. In this book, we want to create an opposite view, one that is strengths based and future focused and that shows how at-risk students can achieve academically within alternative education programs and in life. Our main aim for this book is to show educators how to practice solution focused brief therapy (SFBT) with at-risk students and how to develop an alternative high school program that follows the change principles and practices that are embedded in the SFBT approach. This book represents our personal desires to see every student succeed and to close the achievement gap. It is our goal to communicate to you proven practices from SFBT that we have learned from many years of work in education, with at-risk students, and in alternative high schools.

We are personally and professionally qualified to speak to the topic of ensuring the academic success of at-risk students. The topic is, in fact, very personal to us all. Dr. Cynthia Franklin was a high school dropout when a teacher told her that she was a good writer, a comment that had a profound impact on her academic self-confidence and ability to graduate and proceed to college. Dr. Calvin Streeter did not start his academic career in a manner that would make most educators predict his later success. An average student in high school, he operated a car repair shop for 10 years before ever setting foot on a college campus. From her childhood, Ms. Samantha Guz graduated from an alternative high school, and her experiences in that school led her to be a social worker because she came to understand the social injustices and mental health issues that are often overlooked in other schools.

Dr. Linda Webb had a personal experience as a young child that she often shares with other educators because it profoundly shaped her perspective and prepared her to work with at-risk students: "Soon it was time for me to leave the security of my daily home life and embark on my school career. My mother assured me that I would enjoy myself and that the teacher would love having such a sweet little angel in her room. The next day, I arrived at the door of Ms. Hancock's room, I saw my name on the door. As the day progressed, Ms. Hancock showed us the star chart. The students' job was to fill up the star chart, she said, with stars earned for demonstrating the ability to count to 100, to identify colors, and to tie a bow, among others. I was excited because I could already do most of those activities. Every day we had a chance to show our classmates what we had mastered and were given a star—in front of everyone. One afternoon, Ms. Hancock brought out a red wooden shoe and asked, "Who would like to earn a star for tying the shoe today?" My hand rocketed up, and my heart pounded with joy when she chose me. I pranced to the front of the room, took one lace, pinched it together to make a loop, and manipulated the other lace around the loop. I bent down and grabbed the shoelace with my teeth to pull it through the loop. "Nasty Girl! What would your mother think of you putting that in your mouth?" bellowed Ms. Hancock. I had no answer. Emotionally shocked and ashamed, I silently retreated to the far end of the carpet and slumped to the floor. As I tried to make myself as small as possible, Ms. Hancock's ramblings about the filthy hands that had touched the laces and about never putting objects in your mouth became unintelligible to me. "Nasty girl" were the only words circulating in my mind. When I looked at the star chart, I never saw the accumulated gold stars. The one blank square, four places from the left, that screamed NASTY GIRL, claimed my focus. During the last week of school, I knew that I would fail kindergarten, and that everyone would discover my nastiness.

At home, I grabbed Teddy, the only creature to whom I had confided my nastiness, and cried as though my heart would break. My big brother entered my room to ask what was wrong. I explained through sobs that I couldn't tie my shoes. "Your shoes are tied, silly goose," he said. Through gulps of air, I managed to utter "school" and "no star." My brother gently asked, "Did you tie your shoes at school the way Mother ties shoes?" Of course! How else would I tie them? Then my brother quietly explained to me that there were certain things we did only in our home. These things were not bad, but other people might misunderstand them. That afternoon, my brother taught me to tie my shoes with my hands. You see, my mother was born without hands, and I had learned to tie my shoes by watching her lovingly tie my sister's shoes and mine. I went to school the next day, tied my shoes "Ms. Hancock's way," and got my star. The illumination of that star still shines throughout my life and guides my teaching philosophy. Through our personal, ignorant judgments of children, we educators can unconsciously, but permanently, clip the innocent wings of angels. I graduated from kindergarten realizing that I should never judge others solely on the basis of my viewpoint of a situation. To discover the real meaning behind others' actions, I must allow others to shine their perspectives on the situation. Doing so sometimes allows me to see a rainbow in what appear to be dark and stormy skies. How sad it would be to go through life thinking there is only one way to tie a shoe!" (Webb, 2016).

Audiences and Contents of the Book

All professionals interested in learning how to practice SFBT with children and adolescents will find the contents of this book to be very interesting and useful to their work. The main audiences for this book are school professionals that work in alternative high schools (e.g., principals, teachers, counselors, social workers) and others who would like to improve the educational practices within alternative schools (e.g., parents, school district officials, school board members). We wrote this book to be very practical and helpful to practitioners who want to learn how to use SFBT with high-risk adolescents in alternative schools. The case examples and experiences of practitioners are interwoven into every chapter of this book and demonstrate how SFBT can be used by everyone in an alternative high school to ensure the academic success and graduation of a variety of high-risk students. Specifically, we provide real case examples from administrators, teachers, counselors, and social workers that show how to practice SFBT from our work in an alternative high school: Gonzalo Garza

Independence High School in Austin, Texas. Garza is a public school of choice that has been in operation since 1998 and has distinguished itself as a solution focused alternative high school program with a proven record in graduating high-risk adolescents and sending them to postsecondary education. Case examples and applications of solution focused techniques are taken from both research interviews and daily practices using SFBT within the alternative high school program.

There are seven chapters in this book. Chapter 1 establishes the origins of SFBT and its effectiveness within schools. It also explains the change processes of SFBT and briefly describes its question techniques (e.g., exception questions, scaling questions, miracle question). It further shows how to translate the change processes of SFBT that are defined in the chapter into an alternative school program by following eight solution focused principles. Chapter 2 was developed based on frequently asked questions from a myriad of practitioners from the United States and other countries, who ask specific questions about how Garza High School was created and operates. Specifically, this chapter addresses how to develop a solution focused mind-set and covers different facets of how to create a solution focused alternative high school program, including the importance of and how to develop a solution focused campus community. Chapter 3 shows the importance of relationships and specifically demonstrates how to build relationships with at-risk students using SFBT. It also shows how important relationships with teachers are to at-risk students. Chapter 4 illustrates how to set goals and positive expectancies, and develop hope and other positive emotions with at-risk students. It also illustrates how to develop a success story inside the alternative high school and how a positive school experience can decrease stress on parents and families. Chapter 5 discusses how to create a solution focused student services team within an alternative high school using an inter-professional and transdisciplinary team approach. Chapter 6 covers curriculum and instruction, showing the major elements needed to educate and graduate at-risk students within an alternative high school program. This chapter also shows how to use goals, solution-building conversations, and other solution focused practices in curriculum and instruction. This chapter further provides numerous examples of how teachers use SFBT questions and techniques in the classroom with at-risk students. Finally, Chapter 7 discusses the topic of how to sustain SFBT within an alternative high school program, providing practical advice for how to navigate changes.

Acknowledgments

First, we would like to thank all the teachers, staff, and students of Garza High School who provided their experiences in the development of this book. We especially want to thank Ms. Coila Morrow whose persistence in working with us on scheduling, interviews, and gathering information from teachers was instrumental in the case studies provided. Our special thanks to all the teachers, counselors, and social workers who wrote down their personal experiences in using SFBT and endured the ongoing interviews about their work. We would also like to thank all of our graduate research assistants, who helped us gather the data, case studies, and the stories that enrich the chapter contents. We especially thank Daniella Allen for her help in gathering information and on earlier drafts of one of the chapters. We also acknowledge the editorial help of Lenore Myka on the manuscript. Additionally, we would like to thank the editors and staff at Routledge, who also worked with us on the manuscript and made the published work possible. Finally, we thank all our families and staff for enduring the process we went through to write the manuscript. It takes a team to develop a book.

Cynthia Franklin
Calvin L. Streeter
Linda Webb
Samantha Guz

REFERENCE

Webb, L. (2016). The Red Shoe. Austin Texas, Linda Webb, PhD. www.youtube.com/watch?v=kiAdwNsEOB4

1

Creating Alternative High School Programs that Are Solution Focused

Imagine a high school where students are in control of their destiny. Imagine a high school that believes that environment and past history do not have to decide a student's future. Imagine a high school that teaches that a student's family problems or neighborhood do not have to dictate personal success in school or work. Imagine a high school that considers a student's personal adversities and life difficulties to be strengths that can be harnessed for the better. Imagine a high school that inspires hope and teaches that the small steps a student takes can lead to big changes in life. Imagine a high school where each principal, teacher, counselor, social worker, and staff member is convinced that every student has capacities that can be built upon to assure a positive outcome for that student. Imagine a high school where at-risk and dropout youths attend school, graduate, and successfully transition to college and work. Imagine a solution focused alternative high school where dreams come true.

Introduction

Alternative education programs encompass public alternatives, charter schools, and other alternative educational programs that fall outside the normal K-12 instruction. They are more relevant than ever, given the current focus of education policy on school choice options. Parowski et al. (2014) report that 48 states and the District of Columbia offer alternative education programs and that the majority of these schools serve students at the middle and high school levels. Studies indicate that alternative school students are more likely to have faced adverse childhood experiences, to be traumatized, and to experience mental health symptoms and behavioral problems. Many alternative school students also experience marginalization and oppression due to discrimination and their ethnic minority and low-income status than students in traditional public schools (Escobar-Chaves, Tortolero, Markham, Kelder, & Kapadia, 2002; Grunbaum et al., 2000). The most common problems of alternative school students are behavioral health, academic underachievement, and truancy (Foley & Pang, 2006). Socioeconomic stress, family issues, and problems such as substance use, adolescent pregnancy, child-rearing, and unstable living arrangements are also common among alternative high school students (Bornsheuer, Polonyi, Andrews, Fore, & Onwuegbuzie, 2011; Breslau, Miller, Chung, & Schweitzer, 2011; Lehr, Tan, & Ysseldyke, 2009).

This book aims to show school administrators, teachers, counselors, social workers, and all other school staff how they can create a solution focused alternative high school that uses the therapeutic change techniques of Solution Focused Brief Therapy (SFBT) to graduate at-risk high school students who are also ready for college. This book draws on both research and practice experiences that demonstrate how to implement SFBT in alternative education. The research comes from a growing body of evidence that shows that SFBT is an effective intervention with children, adolescents, and young adults in schools, clinics, juvenile courts, and child welfare settings (Bond, Woods, Humphrey, Symes, & Green, 2013; Franklin, Kim, & Tripodi, 2009; Franklin, Trepper, Gingerich, & McCollum, 2012; Jordan et al., 2013). The practice experiences come from actual work using SFBT within an alternative high school: Gonzalo Garza Independence High School (hereafter referred to as "Garza"), located in Austin, Texas. Garza has been using SFBT since 2001 and is referred to as a solution focused high school because all of the staff there use SFBT practices to help at-risk students graduate.

The beginning chapter of this book describes the origins of SFBT and how it is used in schools. The change processes and techniques of SFBT are also described and illustrated. This chapter further demonstrates how the change techniques embedded in SFBT can be translated into an alternative high school program by carefully adhering to a set of solution focused principles that can be used by everyone in the alternative high school. When school staff practice these principles, a team and school culture is created that helps at-risk students graduate.

SFBT in Schools

SFBT was developed by an interdisciplinary team of mental health professionals led by two social workers, Steve de Shazer and Insoo Kim Berg, at the Brief Family Therapy Center in Milwaukee, Wisconsin during the early 1980s (de Shazer, 1985; de Shazer et al., 1986). The interdisciplinary-team approach took center stage in the development and practice of SFBT. With the aid of a one-way mirror, different therapists and researchers interacted with one another and with children, adolescents, and families who came to the clinic in live consultations. Many families come to therapy with personal traumas and a multitude of problems, such as homelessness, child abuse, mental illnesses, and substance use as well as frequent contacts with social services and court systems. The Milwaukee therapy team found that having conversations with family members about their strengths and resources, past successes, and goals and future hopes worked better than exclusively talking about their past problems and trying to develop strategies to solve those problems. This strengths-based and future-oriented way of helping people solve their problems became core to the therapeutic change processes of SFBT. Over time, therapists and researchers improved and studied the therapeutic techniques of SFBT and demonstrated in research studies that it is an effective method for working with children and adolescents (Franklin et al., 2012).

Counselors and social workers started using SFBT in schools during the early 1990s, and from that work, conceptual and practice publications followed (e.g., Berg & Shilts, 2005; Kelly, Kim, & Franklin, 2008; Kral, 1995; LaFountain & Garner, 1996; Metcalf, 2008; Murphy, 1996; Murphy & Duncan, 2007; Sklare, 1997; Webb, 1999). Research studies showed that SFBT was a useful approach to ameliorating emotional and behavioral issues, such as anxiety, depression, and substance use; conduct problems; and academic problems, and that it helped with dropout prevention (e.g., Bond et al., 2013; Franklin, Biever, Moore, Clemons, & Scamardo, 2001; Franklin, Moore, & Hopson, 2008; Franklin, Streeter, Kim, & Tripodi, 2007; Kim & Franklin, 2009; Newsome, 2004). SFBT has been used effectively in schools with underserved, economically disadvantaged, and ethnic minority students (Kelly & Bluestone Miller, 2009; Newsome, 2004), and research studies demonstrated that SFBT can be effectively used among diverse populations (Fong & Urban, 2013; Hsu & Wang, 2011; Kim, 2013).

As a result of over 30 years of study, SFBT is now an accepted intervention in school social work and counseling, and is being applied across disciplines (e.g., counseling, school social work, and psychology) within schools in the United States, Canada, Europe, Australia, South Africa, Korea, and in the provinces of Mainland China and Taiwan (e.g., Daki & Savage, 2010; Fitch, Marshall, & McCarthy, 2012; Kelly et al., 2008). It is an appropriate intervention for schools because it can be used in Tier 1 interventions by teachers in the classroom as well as in Tier 2 and Tier 3 interventions by counselors and social workers, and other mental health professionals (Franklin & Guz, 2017; Metcalf, 2010). SFBT interventions have been applied at different grade levels and with varying groups (e.g., teachers, parents, and students). Research has also shown that it can be delivered in different modalities, including individual, group, classroom, family, and even organizational-level interventions.

The Importance of Teachers Learning SFBT

Teacher-student relationships are important to all school mental health interventions and ultimately to the success of schools (Paulus et al., 2016). Research shows that teachers commonly address the majority of challenging behaviors in the classroom (Barnes et al., 2014), making their role with at-risk students in alternative education especially significant for ensuring success. A strength of SFBT is that it can be taught to all instructional personnel in an alternative high school and not just to specialized instructional support personnel who have more training in counseling. Even though no one expects teachers to become therapists, anyone in the alternative high school can be taught how to have a solution-building conversation with at-risk students and to follow the basic change processes and techniques of SFBT. Research shows that teachers are effective in the delivery of Tier 1 mental health interventions in the classroom, but many of the interventions are highly structured and are presented as curriculums on social skills and so forth (Franklin et al., 2017). While structured curricula can be useful, SFBT offers a more flexible approach by helping teachers learn how to have a conversation with students using its change processes and specific techniques, which include knowing how to listen and ask the right kinds of questions. Solution focused conversations do not depend on a lesson format but instead can be held spontaneously when problems arise. Even in unexpected crisis situations, teachers will know how to respond using SFBT practices. SFBT interventions are also structured enough that they can be built into other counseling interventions and daily academic processes within the classroom, such as identifying student strengths and setting daily and postgraduation goals.

Understanding the Change Processes and Therapeutic Techniques of SFBT

SFBT has firm grounding in scientific research within the social and psychological sciences, and uses proven methods from communication and cognitive sciences, sociology, and psychology. Since this book is intended to be practical, we will not discuss in detail the theoretical basis of SFBT but instead refer interested readers to authors who have discussed the theoretical origins and research basis for SFBT practice (e.g., Bavelas, 2012; Dejong, Bavelas & Korman, 2013; Franklin, Guz & Bolton, in press; Kim et al., 2015, Lipchik, 2002). Some basic assumptions of SFBT, however, are essential to a foundational understanding for how it works to help at-risk students.

Theoretical Assumptions of SFBT

SFBT views individual change as being relational and contextual, and focuses on the whole student and all the systems that envelop him or her (e.g., family, neighborhood, school, work). SFBT views problems as interactive, which means that problems are defined and solutions happen in social relationships between people. School problems are solved when people communicate, work together, and agree that solutions have been demonstrated. Such assumptions are foundational to brief family systems therapies, therapies based on social constructionism and communication sciences, and other counseling approaches that rely on ecological systems theory. No one solution is believed to fit everyone or every problem. In fact, the same solution may work with different problems or result in novel outcomes. At the same time, very different and unique solutions may lead to the same desired outcomes. For this reason, school staff work with an individual student and relevant systems to individualize and personalize resources and curricula to develop goals and academic solutions.

SFBT believes that it is important to focus on the strengths and resources of people, and to remove negative labels. This means not pathologizing student behavior and avoiding talking in ways that are absolute and offer no choices or ways out of problems. This is sometimes referred to as *no option talk* or talking in a way that does not acknowledge choices and possibilities for student progress. In a solution focused perspective, not pathologizing student behavior involves avoiding labels, such as *hyperactive* and *troublemaking*, as absolute terms or in ways that define that person. Instead, the student would be discussed as being more than that label, and conversations would be directed toward helping them choose ways of acting that can improve their life, even though they may have some limitations. By not directing labels or negative descriptions at students or using these in the presence of a student, teachers and other staff are letting students know that staff value who they are and what they bring to the classroom. No option talk includes words such as *never*, *always*, and *can't*. Examples of no option talk would be "She never sits in her seat" or "He can't stay organized." No option talk focuses on the problem rather than the solution and does not fully describe and accurately portray what the student does. For example, "She sits for ten minutes in art" is a far more accurate description than "She never sits in her seat." For the student that "never" seems organized, it is important to take note of the fact that although he has difficulty bringing his homework in for this afternoon class, he does okay in the morning for first-period class. The focus on strengths and the removal of negative labels and stigmas are related to social constructionism and other strength-based perspectives on counseling.

SFBT uses collaborative language theory from the communication sciences whose scientific study has shown that conversations are negotiated and co-constructed between people, resulting in a therapeutic process known as the *co-construction of meaning*. SFBT purposefully uses conversations to shift the meanings and future behaviors of people toward positive interpretations and solutions. This process helps people see something different about themselves and others, and construct a different story about what they are able to do and further helps them do more of what works or do something totally new. The philosophical, post-structural views of language, such as Ludwig Wittgenstein's language games, have also been discussed in relation to how language and meaning work in this type of perceptual shift between people during a conversation. Wittgenstein believed, for example, that the meanings of words are established through rules created over the course of social exchanges in a conversation and that definitions of words can not be understood outside the social context in which words are grounded between the participants. This perspective represents a complicated pattern of interactions. But understood simply and for the purposes of solution focused alternative schools, staff must watch what they say, paying close attention to how words are used with students. The implications are that language is not neutral and that the questions staff ask may ultimately determine how problems are constructed and solved (Franklin et al., 2017).

The co-construction process is happening constantly between people when they talk and is a type of mutual influence that affects how people understand themselves and others, and their situations. The meanings of words themselves are defined between people in a negotiated conversation process that is sometimes referred to as grounding the conversation in a way that may change how both people perceive what is being discussed. Perhaps you have thought about this process in relation to extreme social interactions, such as a mob mentality; however, in any conversation, people can provoke and evoke meaning and actions from one another. This means that during communication, people are subtly teaching and influencing the perceptions of one another. Co-construction is essential to how SFBT helps people change, and this approach to counseling uses purposeful language to help at-risk students discover solutions that will improve their lives. SFBT uses the co-construction process and language as a vehicle for change, and what this means is that change is constantly happening during the conversations, and the counselor, social worker, teachers, and others are purposefully using the conversation to build hope and competencies and to guide the person toward a solution (de Shazer, 1994). SFBT therapists specifically use a counseling technique that is grounded in the way that language normally works, called Listen, Select, and Build, to help people change their perspectives and direct their behaviors toward a solution. Using these techniques, the therapist listens carefully to what the person says and selects what they say that guides them toward the preferred future. Using this approach, the therapist purposefully builds upon the at-risk student's own language to define and discuss what the preferred future will look like and how they will make it happen (De Jong & Berg, 2013). During Listen, Select, and Build, the at-risk adolescent's own understandings and words are used as a starting point for co-constructing new meanings, and this is an important step to co-construction. This process of listening and purposefully selecting words that help build solutions will be illustrated later.

What Alternative High School Staff Need to Know to Be Able to Practice SFBT

When applied in an alternative education among diverse staff, SFBT is called a solution-building conversation. This de-emphasizes the therapeutic, something associated with the domain of counselors, social workers, and other therapists. As mentioned, the change process of SFBT happens in normal conversations between people and is assisted by an in-depth understanding of how solution focused therapists can purposefully orchestrate these conversations to build solutions. In order to be able to conduct solution-building conversations in alternative education, all school staff, not just those trained in social work and counseling, need to be able to carry out the solution-building conversation by following the change processes of SFBT. While teachers are not expected to have the advanced clinical expertise of therapists in the school, it is assumed that anyone can learn the basic elements required to carry out the solution-building conversation and to apply the techniques to the best of their abilities. Teachers and principals can learn these techniques, for example, with the help of mental health professionals. In the following, we discuss some of the important elements of the SFBT change processes.

Cooperative Relationships

All school staff need to be able to use SFBT to create cooperative and empowering relationships with at-risk students. Relationships are important to all therapeutic change. Adam Froerer and Elliott Connie (2016) discuss how the therapeutic alliance and relationships in SFBT are client led. This means that social workers, counselors, and teachers closely follow the student's lead and use active, intentional, and selective listening to collaborate with the student toward a solution. This process is analogous to a slow dance or following a partner for a while and then taking the lead. This process is sometimes also referred to as "leading from one step behind." When using SFBT, the school staff focus on understanding and respecting the person's feelings and viewpoint, and on listening closely for what the student wishes to be different (goals). Staff members also actively and intentionally listen for strengths, resources, and competencies that the student possesses or would like to learn, that is, the things the student is capable of doing based on past experiences and/or new behaviors they want to learn or experiment with in the future. It is also important to keep in mind that communications are both verbal and nonverbal; silence and body language can speak volumes.

The techniques of Listen, Select, and Build that were described are important to keep in mind. Using these techniques, the school staff summarize what is being heard and asks questions in ways to solicit from the student exceptions to problems, hopes and competencies, and goals and solutions. These techniques provide a reciprocal approach for increasing a cooperative relationship and building a solution. For example, after intentionally listening to a student discuss a problem of failing a math class, by carefully selecting the words and parts of the student's story in which they noticed a strength, a teacher might say,

> I heard you say that even though you 'failed math' that you 'kept going to the class.' Then the teacher may build upon what was said. What I notice about you is you are able to keep trying even though it is so frustrating for you. You kept going to the class when there is no way you can pass. How did you learn to be so persistent?

This ending question begins to shift the conversation toward the competencies of a student that may move them toward a solution. Box 1.1 shows another example of a solution-building conversation, which was taken from an excerpt in a case from a social worker, Jack Nowicki, who worked with an at-risk adolescent and her mother. This family situation is similar to the types of cases in which SFBT was developed and is also typical of the type of family situations that might be encountered in alternative education. In fact, in the past, Nowicki has been involved in training sessions at Garza High School. In this case, a 15-year-old female was brought in to a Youth & Family Resource Center by her mother after the mother had picked the daughter up from the juvenile detention center. The mother had gotten into a physical altercation with the youth, which ended in the police being called. The girl was placed overnight at the detention center, and the mother was reported to Child Protective Services (CPS) for child abuse. Then the detention center released the daughter to the mother and directed her to a crisis counseling center for a counseling session. In the crisis session, the social worker in this case is actively and selectively listening for exceptions to problems that can be the basis for building a solution. Note how the words and questions of the social worker are selected in ways that shift the conversation toward goals, change, and solutions. It is through this process that you can also see how the meanings are co-constructed in ways that move the conversation toward positive emotion, a different perspective on the problem, and a solution.

Box 1.1 A Solution-Building Conversation: The Daughter, the Mother, and the Grandmother

Mother:	"First that little bitch gave me an attitude after school and when I told her to go to her room, she flipped me off and started to walk out the door. I ran over and grabbed her by the arm and she yelled at me and called me some names I can't say here, and tried to hit me. So I slapped the crap out of her."
Social Worker:	"So, you all were in a fight by then." I turned to the daughter and asked, "So, is that pretty much the way you remember it too?"
Daughter:	(Hesitating, and then looking down at the floor) "Yeah. I guess so."
Social Worker:	"Huh. So, you both agree on the story. That's good. What happened next?"
Daughter:	(Looking over at her mother, who nodded agreement that she should continue) "Um... well I just ran out and she yelled at me she was calling the police." (Looking back at the floor again)
Mother:	"You didn't tell him about kicking me almost over before you ran out!" To me: "So I did call the cops and told them she ran away when I was trying to discipline her. They had a car right around the corner and they got her and brought her back and I told them to keep her; she couldn't stay here!"
Social Worker:	"Okay. So has this kind of crisis ever happened before? (Both nodded that it hadn't) Okay. So what do you want to accomplish here today?"

(Continued)

(Continued)

The youth looked back down at the floor, and her mother continued:

Mother:	"I want her out of my house. She can't treat me like that and live with me. Every time I try to tell her anything, she flips me off, cusses in my face, rolls her eyes, and then just goes off and does whatever she wants. I won't put up with it any more!"
Social Worker:	"Hmmm. Is there ever a time that she doesn't act like that when you make a request of her? Or, is there ever a time when it doesn't seem to bother you as much?"
Mother:	(Quickly) "No sir. I try to be a good mom and treat her right and this is what I get. It used to not be so bad when she was younger, but now that she's bigger SHE KNOWS everything!" (Staring at the daughter, who is still looking at the floor)
Social Worker:	"So, aside from when she was younger, there's never a time when it's any better at all…" (The youth looks up slightly and says in a quiet voice to me)
Daughter:	"I don't cuss at Grandma's house."
Social Worker:	(Showing curiosity) "You don't curse at your grandma's house? Huh." (To the mother) "Did you know that? Have you ever noticed she does better when you are at… Is it your mother's house?"
Mother:	"Yeah. We don't even see cussing at my mother's house. Hum. I guess she DOES do better over there. She is usually playing with the little nieces and outside or watching TV."
Social Worker:	"Wow! So how did you get her to act so good at your mother's house? How does she do that and what have you taught her about respecting her grandma?"
Mother:	"I don't think I did anything. It is up to her. She knows she better act good over there!"
Social Worker:	"Well, how did you teach her to do that? I think you must have had some positive influence…"
Mother:	"Well, I guess I act better there too. I wouldn't blow up at her in front of my mom! (And they both smiled)."

Source: Case material from Jack Nowicki, MSSW, LCSW, Adjunct Professor, Steve Hicks School of Social Work, The University of Texas at Austin. Used with Permission.

Solution-building conversations that use the techniques of Listen, Select, and Build will result in forming a helpful relationship that can lead a student to feel understood and cared for (Froerer & Connie, 2016). Chapter 2 of this book is dedicated to discussing how teachers and other school staff can use SFBT to build cooperative and empowering relationships with at-risk students.

Focus on Solutions and Not on Problems

A solution is a future-oriented social action and defines the next steps one will take in relation to and with other people. Solution focused strategies enlist the expertise of the student to identify an existing solution. This entails being able to visualize what the student and others can do immediately or in the future that will result in a different set of relationships and outcomes that the student wants to achieve. Instead of spending time rehashing problems and trying to brainstorm alternatives to get rid of them, school staff and students are focused on describing what a solution looks like, steps and details for achieving it, and what small ways the solution may already be happening in the student's life. Educators ask us if solution-building is just the same as the problem-solving approach that school staff already use. While problem-solving can be an extremely effective approach, solution-building is different than problem-solving, and there is research that shows that the two approaches differ in therapeutic methods of change and outcome (Jordan, Froerer, & Bavelas 2013; Richmond, Jordan, Bischof, & Sauer 2014). We can say with certainty that the solution-building process has to be learned and that the focus of solution-building solves problems but is philosophically and procedurally different than problem-solving. It is important for school staff to understand the importance of focusing on solutions in conversations instead of problems because there are advantages to using solution-building instead of problem-solving when working with at-risk students.

Why Solution-Building Works Better than Problem-Solving

There are five reasons why solution-building may work better than problem-solving when working with at-risk students in alternative education. First, while using approaches to problem-solving, adults often act as experts who educate and tell students what to do, but in solution-building, students become the experts and are asked to build their own solutions and take responsibility for their own education and outcomes. You may be familiar with the fact that telling people what to do may not lead to positive, lasting behavioral changes. Anyone who has ever been told to go on a diet or pursue better eating habits can relate to the challenges. Many at-risk students have problems with attachment and relationships that may cause them to have difficulties with authority figures and in trusting relationships. Working on problems from a solution-building approach circumvents some attachment and relational problems with at-risk students by not taking the expert stance that educates and directs them to find answers to their problems in an authoritarian manner. While it is important for students to accept direction and for relational abilities to improve, the resolution of attachment problems can be lifelong and may not be solved briefly in a class at school. The collaborative approach to relationships that is used in SFBT versus the expert approach of problem-solving can be useful in alternative education in navigating relationships by showing school staff how to increase cooperative and trusting relationships. Many students who attend alternative education may be used to relying on themselves and even taking care of others because they come from families in which parents are absent, overly stressed, or have mental illnesses. The opposite pattern may also be observed, in which students are overly dependent and have been hampered from taking responsibility for themselves by intrusive, enabling, overbearing, or overanxious parental figures. Everyone in schools these days recognizes the term "helicopter parent" and what that means, for example.

For all of these reasons, it is important for adults within the school to create a cooperative relationship by cooperating with students' unique styles of learned interactions. Many students, for example, may not trust adults, causing them to not follow instructions or to avoid having a close relationship. Of course, adults do not like this style of interaction because it can be seen as rebellious and confrontational or passive aggressive. In another example, some students may be sensitive to rejection and not trust adults because of adverse childhood experiences or discrimination. When adults try to direct them toward problem-solving, they resist and reject those efforts. Using SFBT, school staff note the unique relational and learning styles of students, focusing on strengths, such as independence and sensitivity to others and the meaning of the injustices in society that students may have experienced. They use the unique experiences and the strengths of students to speak to them with respect and affirmation. Students, in return, are asked to provide the same kind of respect. It is important to acknowledge the student's experiences as valid and true and, instead of pointing out problems, to draw on their strengths and experiences in building solutions. School staff using SFBT further hold students accountable for their own solutions using natural consequences and caring feedback, and this can facilitate a more trusting atmosphere.

Second, solution-building may work better than problem-solving because at-risk students may exaggerate problems, and this can lead to feelings of hopelessness and despair. Some students magnify how horrible everything is and may even blow their problems out of proportion. This can make them and everyone else feel hopeless when discussing a problem. Students may even learn to like the negative attention that talking about the problem brings. This blocks a solution. SFBT short-circuits the exaggeration of problems by focusing on student strengths and small steps forward.

Third, problem talk evokes negative emotions that may keep students from seeing and seeking imaginative and creative solutions. Solution talk on the other hand opens up possibilities for solutions. It is not uncommon for students who repeat problem patterns to appear to be stuck on an emotion, like anger or anxiety. When talking about problems, you can witness the negative emotion increasing. While some therapists may see emotional catharsis as useful, SFBT instead focuses on increasing positive emotions and new ways of looking at problems that may help students see ways out of problems and lead them toward new actions that amplify behavior toward a solution. You have probably heard the phrase "analysis is paralyses"; this is closer to the approach of SFBT that limits constant analysis of problems in favor of talking about strengths and solutions. This is not meant to say that problems are not discussed in detail, but it means instead that in order to build a solution, the student needs to move beyond being stuck in the complaining and problem talk toward a new way of feeling and acting.

Fourth, rehearsing problems is often associated with worry, ruminations, rigid thinking, fear, and faulty problem-solving. Common types of faulty problem-solving include avoidance, minimizing or denying the problem, or maintaining an attachment or defense of the problem. The latter is often done by saying that it is not a problem or blaming someone else for why the problem exists. It is my mama's fault, teachers fault, or baby daddy's fault, for example. We are sure you have heard some version of this faulty problem-solving style. Direct problem-solving can sometimes even increase these patterns of behavior, and students can get stuck in one or more of these negative patterns. Old habits for approaching problems can also be hard to break. A solution-building approach focuses on breaking old patterns of thinking and behavior by examining new patterns of behavior needed for the solution to occur. This challenges the student to think and act differently and to practice solutions to problem interactions.

Fifth, solution-building can be more effective than problem-solving because some problems cannot be easily solved. Many problems that students face may not be solvable but are instead defined as perpetual issues, such as adolescent pregnancy, a chronic health condition, or a persistent personality trait. SFBT normalizes these problems as a part of life and helps students accept themselves and their circumstances. A solution-building approach also considers a student's coping abilities. Some students may feel overwhelmed by many adverse childhood experiences and multiple problems; therefore, the problem-solving approach leaves them feeling hopeless, paralyzed, and unable to dig out of their past. SFBT helps these students by moving them forward from where they are and focusing on the future. Focusing on solutions instead of problems is not usually an easy process for educators who have been thoroughly educated in the problem-solving method. To maintain a solution-building approach requires mindfulness and ongoing training. Methods for training and sustainment of solution-building in an alternative high school are more thoroughly illustrated in Chapters 2 and 7.

Focus on the Student's Goal

A solution-building conversation identifies a student's goals and fosters hope and positive expectancies that the student can achieve his or her goals. Within a solution focused perspective, school staff look for goals that are measurable, noticeable, and produce small changes in student behavior. Goals should be self-determined and include hard work, personal responsibility, and commitment. As small changes occur, students are acknowledged for their efforts. For example, notes may be given to students or sent home to parents, or a staff member may share a student's accomplishment with another staff member. It is always important for staff to begin where the student is and to start the solution-building conversation with a question about the student's goal. Examples of such questions posed to students might include, "What are your best hopes for what can happen?" or "What specifically do you want to be different?" It is equally important for staff to be ready for students to react to a solution-building conversation with a problem description but through the process of conversation move toward an understanding of the students' goals. This requires staff members to be patient and provide gentle nudges for students to talk about their goals instead of their problems. For example, the teacher might say, "Tell me again, what would you be doing different once the problem was solved?" Once the goal is established, it is important to frequently circle back around to it as a point of reference for the desired change.

Use the Co-Construction Process and Solution Focused Questions

As has been discussed, the co-construction process is at the core of SFBT and involves collaborative communication in which speaker and listener work together to negotiate meanings. This joint effort, in turn, acts to provide information that shifts meanings and social interactions (Bavelas et al., 2013). According to the SFBT treatment manual, students are specifically asked to co-construct a vision of a preferred future and draw on their past successes, strengths, and resources to make that vision a part of their everyday lives (Franklin et al., 2017). The key change techniques in SFBT involve the purposeful use of questions to facilitate the co-construction process. Researchers have shown how specific questioning techniques (e.g., miracle questions, scaling, relationship questions) are an important means of facilitating changes (e.g., Beyebach, 2014). Box 1.2 illustrates several of the questions that are used in SFBT. It is important for teachers and other school staff to become proficient in asking solution focused questions. The types of questions to ask are further illustrated in other chapters of this book.

Box 1.2 Using Solution Focused Questions

Exceptions to the problem. The school staff identify times when the problem does not occur, effective coping responses, and the contexts for the absence of the problem. The school staff say something, such as,

> Even though this is a very bad problem, in my experience, people's lives do not always stay the same. I bet that there are times when the problem of being sent to the principal's office is not happening or at least it is better. Describe those times. What is different? How did you get that to happen?

The staff gather as many exceptions to the problem pattern as possible by repeatedly asking the client, "What else...? What other times...?" Once an exception has been identified by the student, school staff use prompts, such as "tell me more about that," to help the student describe in detail the exceptions. The staff also use his or her own positive emotions, tone, and intense attention to the student's story to communicate to the student that the staff member is very interested in those exceptions. Such nonverbal gestures as nodding, smiling, leaning forward, and looking surprised are used. The staff also may say something such as "how about that," "I am amazed," or "Wow!" as social reinforcement to the student. This encourages the student to talk on and to develop in more detail the exceptions story.

Scaling Questions. Scaling questions assess the problem and measure the progress toward solutions. A school staff, such as a principal, says,

> On a scale of 1 to 10, with 1 being that you are getting in trouble every day in class, sleeping, and 10 being that instead of sleeping you are doing your work, and your teacher says something nice to you, where would you be on that scale now?

With children and adolescents, smiley and sad faces or other graphics are also used to anchor the two ends of the scale, as is indicated in an example from a teacher at Garza High School. Mr. Fang had been using scaling questions for a while in his classrooms. As a math teacher, he liked to check in on his students and assess their motivation. For

(Continued)

(Continued)

him, scaling questions were a fast way to do that. The students were simply handing in a quarter sheet of paper with the scale on it:

Weekly Check-In

1 5 10

Mr. Fang used this scale as a motivation check-in but also to alert him to what his students needed from him. For example, if a student consistently marked a smiley face on the scale and suddenly gave herself a 5, that alerted Mr. Fang that the student needed a consultation with him.

Mr. Fang's use of scaling questions evolved over his years of teaching. In the beginning, he used a numerical (1–10) and gave the scale out on Mondays. However, over the years, he decided to simplify the scale and mark fewer numbers on it. He found that having a frowning face and a smiley face were clearer ways of asking what he wanted to know from his students. Additionally, he realized that asking for a check-in at the beginning of the week did less to help motivate the students than asking for the check-in on Friday. For example, if he took this information on Monday, he was assessing how they felt at the start of the week before they had begun working toward that week's goal rather than at the end of the week, after five days of work. The benefit of asking at the end of the week is that is allowed Mr. Fang to see how content the students were with their week's work. This knowledge helped him understand how to assist them to set goals in the future.

Other uses of the scaling technique in SFBT include the following: (1) asking questions about where the student is on the scale in relation to solving the problem; (2) using the scaling experience to find exceptions to problems, such as saying, "How did you get to the 3?" or "What are you doing so you are not a 1?"; and (3) employing scales to construct "miracles" or to identify solution behaviors. For example, a school staff, such as a counselor, inquires as to where the client is on the scale (with 1 representing low and 10 representing high). The counselor then proceeds to ask the student how he or she will get from a 1 to a 3. Or the counselor inquires how the student managed to move from a 4 rating to a 5 rating, for example, by asking, "How did you get that to happen? What new behaviors did you implement or what was different in your life that made the changes?" Solution focused practitioners may also express surprise that the problem is not worse on the scale as a way of complimenting the student's coping behavior or as a way to use language to change the client's perception of the intractable nature of the problem.

Coping and motivation questions. This is a variation on the scaling question that helps the school staff assess the student's motivation for solving the problem as well as how well the student perceives that he or she is coping with the problem. A school staff, like a school social worker, may say something like,

> On a scale of 1 to 10, with 10 being that you would do anything to solve this problem, and 1 being that you do not care so much for solving it, where would you say you are right now?

Or the social worker may say,

> On a scale of 1 to 10 with 1 being that you are ready to throw in the towel and give up ever doing well in school, and 10 being that you are ready to keep on trying, where would you rate yourself right now?

After asking coping and motivation questions, the social worker should be able to determine the following:

a If the problem that has been defined is too overwhelming to the student. If the problem is too overwhelming, then the problem needs to be broken down into smaller steps and redefined for the student.
b How much self-efficacy and hope the student possesses toward the problem resolution. If the student does not believe the problem can be solved, steps must be taken to change this belief. Here, the exception questions can be empowering.
c What is the degree of commitment to work on the problem? If the student is not interested in committing to working on the problem, then the problem must be redefined to muster some degree of commitment.
d If the problem that has been defined is the one that really interests the student and if it is a priority for him or her.

(Continued)

(Continued)

Miracle questions. A teacher says, for example,

> Let's suppose that an overnight miracle happened, and your problem disappeared; but you were sleeping and did not know it. When you woke up the next day, what would be the first thing that you would notice that would be different?

The teacher proceeds to help the student envision how things could be different. An extreme amount of detail is elicited to help develop a set of solution behaviors that are concrete and behaviorally specific. The miracle question helps the school staff and the student to assess a detailed description of the client's perception of what life would be like without the problem. It also helps the staff co-construct with the student a specific set of behaviors, thoughts, and feelings that can become a solution. Ultimately, the school staff can help the student discover a goal and assess what is most important to the student concerning which changes are most important.

Relationship Questions. A relationship question asks students to think about their problems and solutions from the perspective of others. What would your teacher do differently when the miracle happens? What would your mother do if you did that instead? What would your teacher say if you turned in your homework? This helps the student view themselves in relation to others. For example, the social worker may ask a reluctant student who says he does not have a problem what the teacher might say if she were to ask the teacher. In building solutions, a relationship question can be important in two ways:

a Relationship questions ask the student to think about problems from the viewpoint of what others are complaining about and saying, providing social perspective-taking to a conversation.
b Relationship questions ask students to think about what others want them to do without directly asking them to change and further direct students toward considering the consequences of interactions, often leading to a more cooperative stance.

Continuously Coach, Cheerlead, and Build on Student Strengths and Competencies

Solution-building conversations are all about the empowerment, strengths, and resources of students and how to cultivate confidence and steps toward success, and achievement in academics and life. A solution-building conversation means looking for the solution in problem talk. It is important that teachers listen and be attuned to small accomplishments or changes being made by the student and point those out by using compliments. Compliments are different than praising behavior or just catching the student doing something good, although these tactics can also be useful and used together with complimenting a student. In SFBT, compliments help students recognize and acknowledge their own positive attributes, such as being able to set a goal; recognizing their own hard work, effort, and motivation; being able to ask for help, etc. In SFBT, for a compliment to work as intended, the student has to affirm that what is being said is true about him or her. The school staff want students to reflect on what is being said about their strengths and to start saying the compliments to themselves and about themselves to others. Chapters 4 and 6 in this book provide specific examples of how to use solution-building conversations to build competencies with at-risk students.

Don't Let the Idea of No Motivation Halt You or Your Students

Solution-building requires an understanding that motivation is situational and begins where your student is, moving forward in small steps from there. School staff that practice SFBT believe that each student wants something and under the right circumstances can get motivated to achieve that desired outcome. Sometimes, teachers and other school staff forget that motivation can be situational. This is noticeable when we say that a student "has too many problems to graduate," "is a hopeless case and a waste of time," or "is not ready to change." Even though we all feel from time to time that students are not that motivated, SFBT asks us to think about what does motivate the student. When we begin where the student is, we will start to see that there is no such thing as no motivation but only different situations.

"A Solution Focused Perspective" in Alternative Education

When students enter a solution focused alternative high school, they enter with more than a transcript and a to-do list to complete in order to earn a diploma. They enter with knowledge, values, interests, challenges, and goals. A solution focused alternative high school does not just help them gain admittance to college or gainful employment; it aims to prepare them to handle life and whatever it may bring. The question is how to get the solution focused change processes and practices into the alternative high school program. That is where the rubber really meets the road. There are eight principles that administrators, teachers, and other staff can embrace to create a solution focused alternative high school:

1 Priority should always be given to individual relationships and relationship building.
2 Faculty and staff should emphasize building the strengths and resources of students instead of focusing on deficits.
3 Faculty and staff should emphasize student choices and personal responsibility.
4 Students should demonstrate an overall commitment to achievement and hard work.
5 Faculty and staff should trust student evaluations and respect student ideas.
6 Faculty and staff should focus on students' current and future success instead of past difficulties.
7 Faculty and staff should celebrate students' small steps toward success.
8 Faculty and staff should rely on goal-setting activities and the immediate progress of students.

These eight principles serve as a guiding philosophy for the solution focused alternative high school program and its curriculum and instruction. The principles should not be practiced in isolation from one another but are most effective when put in operation together and by everyone within the school. This means that the actions of faculty and staff cannot just be a matter of mental assent toward the principles but must demonstrate a genuine and heartfelt commitment to carrying out each one in faculty and staff interactions with one another and with students.

The solution focused principles sound simple, but it takes commitment and practice to follow each one. No one will be able to practice these principles perfectly, but a continuous effort pays off. Let's take student strengths and relationships, for example. It is easy to give lip service to the idea of working with student strengths, and most teachers, counselors, and social workers would wholeheartedly agree with this idea. The question is how to carry out the strengths perspective while working with diverse students within a school. It is natural to judge some students as incapable and to write them off as incorrigible and unteachable. Teachers may know the importance of having an individual relationship with students. But it is much harder to put strengths and relationships into action when students appear to have a slew of problems as well as a mental health diagnosis.

Take the case of Jonathan, for example, who came to the solution focused alternative high school Garza with a diagnosis of obsessive compulsive disorder. Jonathan spent a lot of time in rituals and muttering to himself. He would not talk to faculty or students in his former school. He was 16 years old and over 6 feet tall. He tended to look down at the floor when spoken to by teachers. He had a pensive and worried look on his face, which sometimes was mistaken for anger. He often stared into space. If you asked him to look at you, he withdrew even more. Jonathan's avoidance of eye contact and his mannerisms caused some teachers to be afraid of what he might do. As a result, in his former school, he had mostly sat alone or in a back room all by himself. Once enrolled in the alternative school, he was very detached, preferred to work on his assignments on the computer, and liked to be left alone.

In the case of Jonathan, it is easier to think about his deficits than his strengths and to feel a bit hopeless and inadequate—even to doubt that you can build a relationship with this student. It is easy for teachers and other staff to transfer these feelings of hopelessness onto one another and even the student. It takes emotional and personal discipline to focus on the strengths and resources of everyone involved and to build a relationship with this student.

Following the principles of focusing on strengths and relationship building, the teachers at Garza asked themselves what might work to help engage Jonathan and get him more involved in the school. They started by observing and trying different interactions with him and looking for something that might work. At first, it appeared that nothing did. But then, one of the teachers noticed that he liked to play games on the computer and would smile and make eye contact with Jonathan when he did. The teacher also discovered that in addition to computers, Jonathan was also interested in films. The school had a communications class that focused on filmmaking, and Jonathan became engaged when the teacher spoke with him about the camerawork. In a few short weeks, he was operating the camera for school events; it was not long before he engaged more with his teachers and peers. Jonathan's diagnosis did not change. But working with his strengths and using the school resources, as well as the continued persistence of teachers to engage him in a relationship, made it possible for him to be more outgoing and involved in the school community.

Let's take a look at another example through the lens of personal choices, student goals, responsibility, and hard work. How do these solution focused principles get transmitted to students within the alternative high school? Joe, a 17-year-old Hispanic student with shoulder-length hair and a large snake tattoo on his left arm, offers a good example. Joe came to Garza with many behavioral problems. He was in constant trouble, skipping school to smoke marijuana with his friends. His chronic absences resulted in his dropping out of his former public school and endless conflict with his father, who wanted to see Joe disciplined and was constantly pressuring him to finish school. Joe initially promised his father he would and agreed to make a new start at the solution focused alternative school. It was not long, however, before he started missing school again, and his absences escalated. At that point, he met with the social worker and principal, who discussed what he wanted to do (his goal) and his choices with him. During this conversation, which was based on solution focused principles, the social worker and principal put Joe in charge of his own actions and emphasized the hard work it would take to make a change. Here is a paraphrase of their conversation based on an interview with the principal and the social worker:

Principal: "Joe, I think Ms. Dangles [the counselor] told you why we are meeting. Your attendance is keeping you from progressing here. It seems you have a tough choice to make."

Joe: "My father and I don't get along and I don't want to keep fighting with him. There is a bunch of problems in my family and they blame me, and if I leave this school it is all going to get worse."

Principal: "What other reasons would make you want to stay in school other than your father and family?"

Joe: "I want to graduate because I want to go to college to become an architect. My dad is the manager of a construction company, and I would like to work in building."

Social Worker: "It is important to you to graduate. So, is that what you want to do?"

Joe:	"Yes, I want to graduate."
Social Worker:	"So, that is not just your dad's goal for you. It is what you want."
Joe:	"Yeah, I want him off my back, but I want to do it too."
Social Worker:	"So, let me understand this. You want to graduate. So, not coming to school keeps you from your goal of graduation."
Joe:	"I guess so."
Principal:	"When you enrolled you told me that you were glad to get another chance to finish school. Is that right?"
Joe:	"Yes."
Principal:	"So, help me understand your decision to not come to school."
Joe:	"Yes, I think being here is another chance because I was a dropout. But, the work is hard here and I like to do other things with my friends on some days. It is like I need a break. I like to work on cars. Anyway, I come back on other days and do my work. I came here because I heard of this school and that you could work at your own pace."
Principal:	"Oh, I see. So you like to spend time with friends instead of coming to school on some days. Of course, coming to school takes hard work, and that might get in the way. Joe, whether you stay now or drop out is really up to you because your attendance is now to the point that you have to decide. Do you want to put the hard work in or is it more important for you to do other things on some days?"
Joe:	"Yeah, I guess I want to stay."
Principal:	"Are you sure? You may want to think about it some more."

Many educators confronting Joe may have approached his situation differently. They may have tried to talk Joe into doing better, expelled him, or called in his dad for leverage. They may have put him on probation or a monitoring system, anything to get him back on track. Instead, the principal and social worker in the solution focused high school put Joe in charge of his own decisions. They worked with the goal he stated and set choices and consequences that he had to confront and take responsibility for. They pointed out how his behavior interfered with his goal. Joe left that meeting and improved at first, but he continued to struggle. Eventually, he did not return to school for a few days. At that point, one of his teachers called to say she understood that he may have decided to leave the school. Joe did not commit one way or another but also did not immediately return to school. After a month, he returned, and his demeanor had changed. He apologized to the principal and social worker and asked if he could please re-enroll. He said he had learned his lesson. After some discussion and an agreement about his attendance, Joe returned, improved his attendance, and graduated. He spoke in a research interview about how lucky he felt that the school took him back and how he made a really bad choice by leaving. He said he had decided to work hard and was very happy to have a second chance, so he could pursue his goal of going to college to become an architect and builder.

Three other related solution focused principles that educators follow are trusting in student evaluations, focusing on the future instead of the past, and celebrating small steps forward. Trusting the evaluations of students does not mean that educators always believe every word out of the mouths of students (this would be naïve) but that students' opinions are considered in the solution-building. Focusing on the future also does not mean that educators are not interested in the problems that students have faced in the past or that they are dealing with in the present because it is important to know each student well (e.g., problem patterns, diagnosis, and life history). Constantly exploring problems, however, is not seen as the best way for educators and students to build solutions. One student enrolled in Garza described how the teachers' practice of solution focused principles had made a big difference, influencing him to move forward with his education:

> I was incarcerated. All these teachers, they came for me. They had my work ready. One of my teachers even drove to the juvenile hall to give me my homework. What kind of school would do that for its students? Most schools would just look at you and say, 'Obviously, you haven't learned your lesson. You're not the kind of student that we need here.' But here they say, 'We still see good in this kid. He may have done bad things but haven't we all.' And when I came back, every teacher gave me a hug.

In this instance, the teachers and other staff focused on the educational progress of the student and the fact that he voiced his personal responsibility for his current situation. They trusted the student's evaluation that despite his problems, he was still interested in finishing his education. Small steps were honored as the student did some of his work while incarcerated. The teachers were also focused on his future success rather than dwelling on his past and present legal problems. This made a big impression on the student, who realized that the way his teachers responded to him was atypical. In this case, even though he had to continue to deal with the consequences of his legal issues, he also returned to the school and continued to make progress.

An Example of Solution Focused Principles in Action

The following is a real-life example, which a teacher at Garza provided for how she used solution focused principles while talking to another teacher:

Math Teacher: "I met with John yesterday to talk about his goals. He wants to graduate next spring, but in order to do that he will have to bring in his homework on time."

English Teacher: "I wasn't aware he was having difficulty bringing in homework for your class. In my class, John consistently has brought his portfolio for our first period morning class this semester."

Math Teacher: "That's interesting. So, he is prepared for his first class period, but struggles being prepared for his afternoon class. I wonder what he does to be prepared for that first period?"

English Teacher: "Yes, it sounds like John has improved since he enrolled here. Now he is prepared for the first class of the day. It seems like he found a solution that works for him. I'll write him a note today to let him know that I see this change."

Math Teacher: "That sounds great. Maybe I can revisit with him and talk to him about that solution."

In this example, two teachers talked about a student struggling to be prepared for class. Rather than complaining about the student and focusing on his problems, the teachers were solution oriented. Instead of labeling the student a problem student with attention deficits who was never prepared, they acknowledged what the student did well for the morning class while recognizing his challenges later in the day. These teachers remained strengths based in their conversation about the student.

Key Points to Keep in Mind

- SFBT has been studied for over 30 years and is a promising and effective intervention with at-risk children and adolescents in schools. All school staff can be trained in SFBT to successfully work with these students.
- SFBT is strengths oriented and future focused and emphasizes goals and future solutions instead of problem patterns. Questions are essential change techniques in SFBT.
- SFBT uses collaborative language theory from the communication sciences, whose scientific study has shown that conversations are negotiated and co-constructed between people. The co-construction process is core to the change processes of SFBT.
- SFBT helps school staff create collaborative and empowering relationships with students.
- Solution-building is different than problem-solving approaches to change. There are several advantages of using solution-building instead of problem-solving with at-risk students.
- When school staff members in alternative high schools practice SFBT change principles and techniques, they are able to create a team and a school culture that helps at-risk students.

Summary

SFBT originated with an interdisciplinary team of mental health professionals working at the Brief Family Therapy Center in Milwaukee, a mental health services clinic, during the 1980s and was adapted into school programs during the 1990s. It is an approach that all school staff can be trained in as a team to successfully work with at-risk students, and this makes it an especially viable approach for alternative education. The change processes and techniques of SFBT were described and illustrated in this chapter, including the types of questions school staff need to learn to ask. In particular, this chapter demonstrated how the change techniques embedded in SFBT can be translated into an alternative high school program by carefully adhering to a set of solution focused principles that can be used by everyone in the alternative high school. When all school staff members practice SFBT, they are able to create a team and a school culture that helps at-risk students. This chapter serves as a beginning chapter on the use of SFBT in alternative education, and the topics introduced in this chapter are discussed and illustrated in subsequent chapters of this book.

References

Barnes, T., Smith, S., & Miller, M. (2014). School-based cognitive-behavioral interventions in the treatment of aggression in the United States: A meta-analysis. *Aggression and Violent Bahavior, 19*(4), 311–321.

Bavelas, J. B. (2012). Connecting the lab to the therapy room: Microanalysis, co-construction, and solution-focused brief therapy. In C. Franklin, T. Trepper, W. Gingerich, & E. McCollum (Eds.), *Solution-focused brief therapy: A handbook of evidence-based practice* (pp. 144–162). New York, NY: Oxford University Press.

Bavelas, J., De Jong, P., Franklin, C., Froerer, A., Gingerick, W., & Kim, J. (2013). *Solution-focused therapy treatment manual for working with individuals* (2nd ed.). Santa Fe, NM: Solution Focused Brief Therapy Association.

Berg, I. K., & Shilts, L. (2005). *Classroom solutions: WOWW approach.* Milwaukee, WI: Brief Family Therapy Center.

Beyebach, M. (2014). Change factors in solution-focused brief therapy: A review of the Salamanca studies. *Journal of Systemic Therapies, 33*(1), 62–77. doi:10.1521/jsyt.2014.33.1.62

Bond, C., Woods, K., Humphrey, N., Symes, W., & Green, L. (2013). The effectiveness of solution focused brief therapy with children and families: A systematic and critical evaluation of the literature from 1990–2010. *Journal of Child Psychology and Psychiatry, 54,* 707–723. doi:10.1111/jcpp.12058

Bornsheuer, J. N., Polonyi, M. A., Andrews, M., Fore, B., & Onwuegbuzie, A. J. (2011). The relationship between ninth-grade retention and on-time graduation in a southeast Texas high school. *Journal of At-Risk Issues, 16*(2), 9–16. doi:20111092657

Breslau, J., Miller, E., Joanie Chung, W. J., & Schweitzer, J. B. (2011). Childhood and adolescent onset psychiatric disorders, substance use, and failure to graduate high school on time. *Journal of Psychiatric Research, 45*(3), 295–301. doi:10.1016/j.jpsychires.2010.06.014

Daki, J., & Savage, R. S. (2010). Solution-focused brief therapy: Impacts on academic and emotional difficulties. *The Journal of Educational Research, 103*(5), 309–326. doi:10.1080/00220670903383127

De Jong, P., & Berg, I. K. (2013). *Interviewing for solutions* (4th ed.). Pacific Grove, CA: Brooks.

De Jong, P. D., Bavelas, J. B., & Korman, H. (2013). An introduction to using microanalysis to observe co-construction in Psychotherapy. *Journal of Systemic Therapies, 32*(3), 17–30.

de Shazer, S. (1985). *Keys to solutions in brief therapy.* New York, NY: W. W. Norton.

de Shazer, S. (1994). *Words were originally magic.* New York, NY: W. W. Norton.

de Shazer, S., Berg, I., Lipchik, E., Nunnally, E., Molnar, A., Gingerich, W., & Weiner-Davis, M. (1986). Brief therapy: Focused solution development. *Family Process, 25*(2), 207–221. doi:10.1111/j.1545-5300.1986.00207.x

Escobar-Chaves, S. L., Tortolero, S. R., Markham, C., Kelder, S. H., & Kapadia, A. (2002). Violent behavior among urban youth attending alternative schools. *Journal of School Health, 72*(9), 357–362. doi:10.1111/j.1746-1561.2002.tb03559.x

Fitch, T., Marshall, J., & McCarthy, W. (2012). The effect of solution-focused groups on self-regulated learning. *Journal of College Student Development, 53*(4), 586–595. doi:10.1353/csd.2012.0049

Foley, R. M., & Pang, L. S. (2006). Alternative education programs: Program and student characteristics. *The High School Journal, 89*(3), 10–21. doi: 10.1353/hsj.2006.0003

Franklin, C., & Guz, S. (2017). Tier 1 approach: Schools adopting SFBT model. In J. S. Kim, M. S. Kelly, & C. Franklin (Eds.), *Solution-focused brief therapy in schools: A 360-degree view of research and practice principles* (2nd ed.). New York, NY: Oxford University Press.

Franklin, C., Biever, J., Moore, K., Clemons, D., & Scamardo, M. (2001). The effectiveness of solution-focused therapy with children in a school setting. *Research on Social Work Practice, 11*(4), 411–434. doi:10.1177/104973150101100401

Franklin, C., Bolton, K., & Guz, S. (in press). Solution-focused brief family therapy. In B. Fiese (Ed.), *APA handbook of contemporary family psychology.* Washington, DC: American Psychological Association Press.

Franklin, C., Kim, J. S., Beretvas, T. S., Zhang, A., Guz, S., Park, S., ... Maynard, B. R. (2017). The effectiveness of psychosocial interventions delivered by teachers in schools: A systematic review and meta-analysis. *Clinical Child and Family Psychology Review, 20*(3), 333. doi:10.1007/s10567-017-0235-4

Franklin, C., Kim, J. S., & Tripodi, S. J. (2009). A meta-analysis of published school social work intervention studies: 1980–2007. *Research on Social Work Practice, 19*(6), 667–677. doi:10.1177/1049731508330224

Franklin, C., Moore, K., & Hopson, L. (2008). Effectiveness of solution-focused brief therapy in a school setting. *Children & Schools, 30*, 15–26. doi:10.1093/cs/30.1.15

Franklin, C., Streeter, C. L., Kim, J. S., & Tripodi, S. J. (2007). The effectiveness of a solution-focused, public alternative school for dropout prevention and retrieval. *Children & Schools, 29*(3), 133–144. doi: 10.1093/cs/29.3.133

Franklin, C., Trepper, T., Gingerich, W. J., & McCollum, E. (2012). *Solution-focused brief therapy: A handbook of evidence-based practice.* New York, NY: Oxford University Press.

Froerer, A. S., & Connie, E. E. (2016). Solution-building, the foundation of solution focused brief therapy: A qualitative Delphi study. *Journal of Family Psychotherapy, 27*(1), 20–34. doi:10.1080/08975353.2016.1136545

Fong, R., & Urban, B. (2013). Solution-focused approach with Asian immigrant clients. *Solution-Focused Brief Therapy: A Multicultural Approach*, 122–132. doi:10.4135/9781483352930.n8

Grunbaum, J. A., Lowry, R., Kann, L., & Pateman, B. (2000). Prevalence of health risk behaviors among Asian American/Pacific Islander high school students. *Journal of Adolescent Health, 27*(5), 322–330. doi:10.1016/S1054-139X(00)00093-8

Hsu, W. S., & Wang, C. D. (2011). Integrating Asian clients' filial piety beliefs into solution-focused brief therapy. *International Journal for the Advancement of Counselling, 33*(4), 322–334. doi:10.1007/s10447-011-9133-5

Jordan, C., Lehmann, P., Bolton, K. W., Huynh, L., Chigbu, K., Schoech, R., ... Bezner, D. (2013). Youthful offender diversion project: YODA. *Best Practices in Mental Health, 9*(1), 20–30. doi:87572266

Jordan, S. S., Froerer, A. S., & Bavelas, J. B. (2013). Microanalysis of positive and negative content in solution-focused brief therapy and cognitive behavioral therapy expert sessions. *Journal of Systemic Therapies, 32*(3), 46–59.

Kelly, M. S., & Bluestone-Miller, R. (2009). Working on What Works (WOWW): Coaching teachers to do more of what's working. *Children & Schools, 31*(1), 35. doi: 1532-8759/09

Kelly, M. S., Kim, J. S., & Franklin, C. (2008). *Solution-focused brief therapy in schools: A 360-degree view of the research and practice principles.* New York, NY: Oxford University Press.

Kim, J. S. (Ed.). (2013). *Solution-focused brief therapy: A multicultural approach.* Thousand Oaks, CA: Sage Publications.

Kim, J. S., & Franklin, C. (2009). Solution-focused brief therapy in schools: A review of the literature. *Children and Youth Services Review, 31*(4), 464–470. doi:10.1016/j.childyouth.2008.10.002

Kim, J. S., Franklin, C., Zhang, Y., Liu, X., Qu, Y., & Chen, H. (2015). Solution-focused brief therapy in China: A meta-analysis. *Journal of Ethnic & Cultural Diversity in Social Work, 24*(3), 187–201. doi:10.1111/jmft.12193

Kral, R. (1995). *Solutions for schools.* Milwaukee, WI: Brief Family Therapy Center Press.

LaFountain, R. M., & Garner, N. E. (1996). Solution-focused counseling groups: The results are in. *Journal for Specialists in Group Work, 21*(2), 128–143. doi:10.1080/01933929608412241

Lehr, C. A., Tan, C. S., & Ysseldyke, J. (2009). Alternative schools: A synthesis of state-level policy and research. *Remedial and Special Education, 30*(1), 19–32. doi:10.1177/0741932508315645

Lipchik, K. (2002). *Beyond technique in solution-focused therapy: Working with emotions and the therapeutic relationship.* New York, NY: Guilford Press.

Metcalf, L. (2008). *A field guide to counseling toward solutions.* San Francisco, CA: Jossey-Bass.

Metcalf, L. (2010). *Solution-focused RTI: A positive and personal approach.* San Francisco, CA: John Wiley and Sons.

Murphy, J. J. (1996). Solution-focused brief therapy in the school. In S. D. Miller, M. A. Hubble, & B. S. Duncan (Eds.), *Handbook of solution-focused brief therapy* (pp. 184–204). San Francisco, CA: Jossey-Bass.

Murphy, J. J., & Duncan, B. S. (2007). *Brief interventions for school problems* (2nd ed.). New York, NY: Guilford Publications.

Newsome, S. (2004). Solution-focused brief therapy (SFBT) group work with at-risk junior high school students: Enhancing the bottom-line. *Research on Social Work Practice, 14*(5), 336–343. doi:10.1177/1049731503262134

Paulus, F. W., Ohmann, S., & Popow, C. (2016). Practitioner review: School-based interventions in child mental health. *Journal of Child Psychology and Psychiatry, 57*(12), 1337–1359.

Richmond, C. J., Jordan, S. S., Bischof, G. H., & Sauer, E. M. (2014). Effects of solution-focused versus problem-focused intake questions on pre-treatment change. *Journal of Systemic Therapies, 33*(1), 33–47.

Sklare, G. B. (1997). *Brief counseling that works: A solution-focused approach for school counselors.* Thousand Oaks, CA: Sage Publications.

Webb, W. H. (1999). *Solutioning: Solution-focused interventions for counselors.* Philadelphia, PA: Accelerated Press.

2

Strategies for Creating a Solution Focused Alternative High School Program

A Story to Get Started

Ximena[1] and her siblings moved in with their aunt and uncle in early January. Over the past several months, her father had one of his limbs amputated due to diabetes complications and was no longer able to serve as guardian. Eventually, he was placed in a hospital and began receiving hospice services. Ximena dropped out of high school her junior year to take a job that would support her father and her siblings. The combination of grief and loss coupled with the transition of moving was difficult for Ximena.

After she moved in with her extended family, Ximena's aunt enrolled her in school and was referred to Gonzalo Garza Independence High School. Ximena had missed her entire junior year of high school and spent much of her time visiting her father in the hospital. It seemed that a traditional school schedule would not meet her needs. Upon beginning classes at Garza, it became clear to Ximena's teachers that she was an incredibly bright student. However, she often had difficulty starting and finishing assignments. It was a confusing case for the teachers; most students who struggled to start and finish assignments had holes in their academic knowledge. However, this was not the case for Ximena.

After a month of classes, a teacher suddenly noticed Ximena's red, puffy eyes. It was clear that Ximena had been crying. She was a student who did not show much emotion, so to see her upset was startling. The teacher immediately referred Ximena to Communities In Schools, a national organization that partners with public schools to offer services on school campuses to help students stay in school. This gave Ximena the option to stay in class and head over to Communities In Schools during lunch or to go over to Communities In Schools immediately, reassuring Ximena that the work she was doing could be addressed later. Ximena took the opportunity to go to Communities In Schools immediately and met with a school social worker. Soon, it became apparent that Ximena was experiencing symptoms of depression: a lack of concentration, feelings of hopelessness, a loss of interest in things that had previously been important to her, an inability to sleep, the sensation of pain throughout her body, and thoughts of suicide.

After a brief session, the social worker and Ximena called Ximena's aunt to inform her of Ximena's symptoms and to ask that she attend regular counseling sessions in school. As a result of ongoing counseling throughout the rest of the school year, Ximena's symptoms improved drastically. She enjoyed her classes more and made some close friends. The slow decline of her father was still difficult for her, but she gained skills to cope with the trauma and grief.

As Ximena moved into her senior year of high school, she asked to remain in counseling at Garza, stating,

> I didn't know about mental health before. Like no one in my family knew what counseling was or that I could get better. I felt that something was wrong with me and I didn't know what to do. I want to stay in counseling because it's still hard for me and I want to take care of myself.

Without the academic and mental health services Garza offered, Ximena may not have been able to receive the counseling she needed to regain stability and graduate high school.

Introduction

Alternative education programs are more relevant than ever, given the current focus of education policy on school choice options. Cynthia

Franklin, Laura Hopson, and David Dupper (2013) describe two different and opposing models of alternative education that have evolved over time. One model is disciplinary or correctional in nature and aims to fix problem students. The second is academic and creative in nature, promoting a more effective way to educate students. A solution focused alternative high school is better aligned with the second approach because it creates a program that is academically rigorous, caring, and supportive as well as one that provides the mental health resources needed to help all students succeed. In fact, a solution focused alternative high school's curriculum and program may resemble elite college preparatory programs more than they would many disciplinary alternative programs that may run similarly to juvenile correctional facilities. This chapter discusses how to develop a solution focused alternative high school program and is based on frequently asked questions about Garza. The need for a solution focused mind-set, which is essential to the development of a solution focused alternative high school, is explained. Practical issues are covered, including examples of how to develop school district and community support, and how to create a leadership team and select the right kind of teachers. People and their relationships are central to a successful solution focused high school, including administrators, teachers, students, parents, community partners, and mental health professionals. This chapter provides examples of how these relationships function in a system to create a campus community that is necessary for student engagement and a school's academic success with high-risk adolescents.

The chapter also discusses the types of at-risk students that are served and how to select and orient those students within a solution focused alternative high school. Finally, this chapter highlights how to train all staff in Solution Focused Brief Therapy (SFBT) and describes how continuous professional development is necessary to assure the success of the school.

Mind-Set Needed to Start a Solution Focused School

In order to start a solution focused alternative school, creators must commit themselves to the mind-set of wanting a real change in education practices, one that is strengths oriented and student centered. The mind-set starts like this: Leaders and staff members must believe that students' attitudes toward education can be changed for the better and that students are able to cooperate toward this change, no matter how horrific the events in their lives may seem. When leaders and staff are ready to show at-risk students that they believe in them and respect them, and want to provide them with the very best education possible, they are in the right mind-set for starting a solution focused alternative high school. The eight solution focused principles discussed in Chapter 1 serve as overarching guidelines that educators can refer back to in creating a solution focused alternative high school program and are repeated here as a reminder:

1 Priority should always be given to individual relationships and relationship building.
2 Faculty and staff should emphasize building the strengths and resources of students instead of focusing on deficits.
3 Faculty and staff should emphasize student choices and personal responsibility.
4 Students should demonstrate an overall commitment to achievement and hard work.
5 Faculty and staff should trust student evaluations and respect student ideas.
6 Faculty and staff should focus on students' current and future success instead of past difficulties.
7 Faculty and staff should celebrate students' small steps toward success.
8 Faculty and staff should rely on goal-setting activities and the immediate progress of students.

We prefer the term solution focused mind-set to communicate what is necessary to help everyone in the alternative high school be able to learn and practice SFBT with confidence and diligence. The phrase solution focused mind-set is best understood through examples. We will start here with an example of a faculty member utilizing a solution focused mind-set:

> Joy Samuels is a middle-aged, short, brunette, Hispanic woman. She has dark eyes and wire-frame glasses, and usually dresses in black pants and long colorful shirts. Ms. Samuels entered her classroom 27 years ago with bright eyes and an eagerness to change her students' world. For many educators, this dream is often brought to a screeching halt amidst the red tape, politics, and lack of cohesive motivation towards a

common goal that may plague schools. However, because Ms. Samuels joined the staff of Garza and was taught solution focused change principles, she has been able to keep her dreams alive.

A few years ago, Ms. Samuels had a student who experienced extreme anxiety in social settings, and having a solution focused approach led both her and her student to a moment of growth. Drawing on her solution focused training, Ms. Samuels asked the struggling student (referred to here as April) a coping question that focused on April's strengths and competencies. The purposeful use of questions with students are essential to changing strategies in SFBT, and the coping question helped Ms. Samuels start a solution-building conversation aimed at helping April think differently about herself in relation to her anxiety and school performance. Ms. Samuels asked, "How did you do it? With all that anxiety, how have you managed in school?" Ms. Samuels wanted April to see that she really had found her own way around her anxiety. By hearing herself say it out loud, Ms. Samuels wanted April to recognize the ways in which she had successfully managed her anxiety. Following the solution focused change principles, Ms. Samuels believed this type of conversation would shift April's perspective toward the recognition of her own competencies and help her feel more hopeful, ultimately guiding her to recognize and utilize her own solutions.

However, 10 minutes later, April was still sharing ways she coped with her anxiety. Ms. Samuels began to feel concerned. Recalling the moment, she said, "The voice in my head said, 'We're talking too long. We should have started our lesson by now.'" She became impatient but then thought to herself, "Our lesson? This is the real lesson!"

When the solution focused mind-set is carried out, space is made for educators to have solution-building conversations with their students in the same way Ms. Samuels had a conversation with April. Leadership should foster a school environment with opportunities for reflection and growth, and should expect these types of discussions to be a part of the everyday communications within the school. The solution focused approach in an alternative school is not a cafeteria plan for educators to pick and choose from a menu of options; it's an approach that works best when it is implemented fully. The solution focused mind-set must extend beyond the individual and permeate into every level of a support system, including administrators, teachers, custodial staff, and cafeteria workers. For the school to be solution focused, every part needs to function as a safe and cohesive system around the students. Teachers and all other staff navigate between interpersonal and social issues, and a self-paced curricular model, which also requires teachers to move across subject areas and know how to implement solution focused principles. This way of operating as a team is necessary to be able to educate and graduate the at-risk students that the school serves. At a school like Garza, the students may have considered or attempted suicide, and many have experienced extreme losses. In addition, a handful may be coming from drug rehabilitation facilities or may be homeless. This creates a fragile bubble around the school, and the solution focused mind-set helps all the staff be prepared to work together to be first responders. At the solution focused alternative high school, the campus community is the first level of intervention. Instead of a police officer, a Child Protective Services (CPS) employee, or a suspension notice, the campus community is the first level of response to a student's need or crisis.

In order to maintain the first level of response mind-set, all staff and faculty members on the campus are trained in SFBT and know how to have a solution-building conversation like the one Ms. Samuels had with April. Additionally, an overarching attitude of trust in and respect for one another should be omnipresent. This is exactly why April, who was normally shy and anxious with others, shared so much with Ms. Samuels. She had built a relationship of trust and respect with April. Ms. Samuels created a safe space for April in which she could take risks and freely express herself. Many students within an alternative high school have adverse childhood experiences that affect their abilities to trust others, and this is why the solution focused high school emphasizes trust and respect in every aspect of its campus community.

Take the case of Heather, who explained in a research interview the two main reasons why she did not trust anyone: her father's abandonment of her and her multiple experiences of rape. The following is an excerpt from a research interview transcript:

Interviewer: "What is the toughest experience you ever faced in your living situation while growing up?"

Student: "I kind of have two but they kind of go together. One was me having to let go of my dad. That was probably the hardest thing ever. Not just my dad leaving and just grieving about that. 'Cause after he left it wasn't just all fine and dandy. OK, my dad's not in my life anymore. Every day you have to think, you know, 'Why did my dad leave? What did I do for that?' Or holidays come and your dad's not talking to you or you can't talk to him. Especially when you're 'Daddy's Little Girl'; that's even worse. And with that, because of him, I've had a lot of hard things with guys. After my dad left I was thinking the only way I could get a guy to love me is having sex with him or doing whatever they want me to do. And being raped twice, that was hard 'cause you know, 'Why am I getting all this horrible treatment from guys? I didn't do anything wrong.' You know it's just real difficult when your dad leaves."

Interviewer: "How old were you when you were raped?"

Student: "I was in the eighth grade so I was 13. And the second time was when I ran away from a residential treatment center, when I was 16."

Interviewer: "Did you ever get any help with these things?"

Student: "The first one was my best friend, so I talked to some people at my school, some cops. And my mom kind of made me feel it was my fault and that I shouldn't press charges 'cause I put myself in that position. The second one I reported it and they didn't believe us—it was me and a friend of mine that both got raped. We didn't know the guy's last name and also the fact that we didn't scream or make any attempt to get out of the situation. And I tried to explain to them when you have a loaded shotgun in the house you're not going to make a sound; you're not going to fight back. Of course, you're going to say no, but you're not going to fight him for it... Because of my dad's absence, and being raped, and having no trust for anybody, especially guys. So it's real hard. And it's something I struggle with every day."

Administrators within a solution focused school lay the groundwork for the solution focused mind-set and restoring trust by modeling respect towards others (such as by wanting to hear the concerns of teachers) and by constantly working with teachers to support them and their work with students like Heather. Every staff member is treated like a member of the campus community, and the culture of the school is one in which everyone supports one another by giving each other individual space to grow professionally. Holding all staff members on campus to the same high standards of respect is crucial to keeping the trust and morale high. While most people will raise themselves to high standards, it is the job of administrators to keep those standards at an appropriate level so that staff members keep reaching for success. Simple things, like starting meetings on time, holding teachers accountable for dressing appropriately, and showing up on time, keep individuals from conducting themselves at lower standards and growing complacent.

This type of approach can help teachers and other staff work through disagreements that might otherwise result in staff working at cross purposes or, even worse, sabotaging each other's efforts. When cooperation occurs between staff, then students will be less likely to successfully divide the staff. This will inevitably result in a calmer and safer atmosphere within the alternative high school. Additionally, when teachers and other staff feel respected and supported in their day-to-day interactions, they are more likely to seek out challenges and to strive for those higher standards. Administrators can show they respect staff, through simple caring interactions, such as offering coffee and water to teachers, and making sure staff members are always putting their family—spouses, children, pets, partners, or friends—first. For example, if staff members need a day off because of a sick pet or child, there is a judgment-free understanding that in order to do their best work they must be taking care of themselves first. By respecting teachers' boundaries, mutual respect between administrators and staff is gained, and staff members can come to work knowing they are valued and supported.

The school's leadership can further foster a respectful, solution focused campus community by asking solution-building questions, like "What made you become a teacher?" "How can I help you remember why you became an educator?" "What makes education work?" "How can I support you so your students will succeed?" and "How can I help you change the world?" Such questions from administrators help staff discuss strengths, renew commitments toward student progress, and keep the solution focused approach foremost in the minds of everyone. One teacher at Garza said,

> Solution focused ideas are not just something you can hear just once; you have to keep reminding yourself so you won't backslide into old ways of talking and interacting. I appreciate that the principal and everyone here supports one another to be solution focused. I discovered that it is a philosophy and a way of life to practice a solution focused conversation. In fact, since I have learned the solution focused approach, it has transformed the relationships in my own family.

Most staff that choose to work in an alternative high school already have the commitment and desire to help that makes it easy for them to renew their commitments to educate and help the students, and to learn SFBT. Ms. Samuels's personal philosophy and caring approach, for example, helped her connect with April, and it was her knowledge of SFBT and a commitment to have a solution focused conversation with students that encouraged her to ask a coping question and to listen. The collaborative leadership from the principal, the professional training events, and staff meetings further facilitate and sustain the solution focused mind-set and participation of the campus community in reflection, exploration, and the practice of a respectful and trusting community. Planned school and community events also provide ample opportunities for staff and students to continuously tap into their passions and creativity in order to revitalize the community around the school. For example, in order to facilitate a campus community, Garza holds community events and invites all of its supporters. A popular community event is "Mix It Up Day," a national movement led by the Teaching Tolerance organization, which is meant to help students "mix up" typical cliques by encouraging students to "identify, question, and cross social boundaries." These types of community events help solidify and sustain the Garza community as a mutual caring and trusting community where every member is supportive of one another.

Creating a Solution Focused High School Program

Once educators are willing to embrace the solution focused mind-set then the practicalities of creating a solution focused alternative high school can be tackled. Many public school districts already have a budget for running alternative and magnet schools. Charter and private schools may want to operate a high school that can graduate students who have similar profiles to those who enter alternative high schools. As in other chapters in this book, in this section we will draw on examples from the solution focused alternative school Gonzalo Garza Independence High School. The issues discussed here are based on frequent questions that have been asked by educators who want to develop a solution focused alternative high school for dropout prevention. While every community has to develop its own unique plan for establishing a school, we believe the examples provided will be instructive.

Finding Support to Start a Solution Focused High School

Practically speaking, alternative high schools exist primarily to support the other schools in their community, providing a space for students who, for various reasons, could not succeed in a traditional high school. These reasons traverse family, behavioral health, and social problem areas that most educators do not feel equipped to handle. Recall from Chapter 1 that the most common problems of alternative school students are behavioral health, academic underachievement, and truancy. Consider Rachel, who graduated from Garza. In her own words, Rachel explained her tragic life situation in a research interview.

Interviewer: "So, where are your parents?"

Rachel: "My parents passed away—about when I was 11. I live with my sister."

Interviewer: "Is your sister much older than you?"

Rachel: "She's 26... Well, actually my father killed my mother and then killed himself."

Interviewer: "Oh, dear. Were you there?"

Rachel: "Actually I was across the street. But my brother was actually in the house when it all happened. But I heard mostly everything."

Interview: "That's really traumatic. Did it happen here in town?"

Rachel: "Happened in the south side of town. It was seven years ago. I had just got out of school; I finished the fifth grade and it happened."

Interviewer: "Your parents died when you were 11, so did your sister kind of become your parental figure?"

Rachel: "Yeah."

Interviewer: "What was the toughest situation growing up?"

Rachel: "Growing up and not having my parents around. Even though I knew I had my sister—my brother—I felt alone... I heard people comment that I wasn't going to finish school, especially when I had a baby—when I found out I was pregnant, everybody said, 'Well, it's over. She's not going to go through with this.' But I did. Proved them wrong. And I had thought I wasn't going to finish school either. But I guess not having my parents, I wanted to do it for them. Even though they weren't here to see it."

It is imperative that the leaders from other high schools believe the solution focused alternative high school can graduate students with life experiences like Rachel's, a girl who was very resilient but whose life circumstances created educational barriers. The solution focused school needs to hold a justified and independent status as a high school that will serve as an educational support program for other high schools in the district.

For another example, let's look at Michael, a black 16-year-old male student who, in his traditional high school, had to repeat the 10th grade and was disruptive in his algebra class. He often bothered other students, and the teacher said she found him intimidating. The teacher spent more time disciplining him than ensuring each student grasped the material they were intended to learn before moving on. Michael spent many hours in the principal's office, was suspended, skipped class, and was in danger of dropping out. The situation left the student and his mother, teachers, and administrators frustrated because Michael's educational goals were not being met.

Michael was referred to Garza by a dropout prevention counselor in his traditional high school. After settling into the small classes and self-paced curricula, the teachers quickly realized that in the past, Michael had missed school because of trauma in his home life and as a result had never learned the building blocks of algebra. Instead of feeling embarrassed or not smart enough, and deflecting these feelings into disruptions, at Garza, Michael was allowed to learn these building blocks at his own pace and succeeded in Algebra I in a smaller, more attentive classroom. Additionally, at his former school, the teacher had more attention to spend on the entire class, the dropout prevention counselor has one less person on his caseload, and the principal's graduation rate potentially rose.

In gathering support for a solution focused alternative school there must be no doubt that it has added value to the wider school community by accepting student referrals from other schools and potentially improving behavior problems, attendance, and graduation rates in those schools. The local school district may benefit from having a solution focused alternative high school where educational solutions are built with students. A solution focused high school helps close the achievement gap by providing a rigorous education to the at-risk students served. We have encountered many educators, mental health professionals, and school reformers who agree with this concept and ask for strategies to convince school and community leaders that a solution focused alternative high school is needed in their areas. They want to know how to market this concept. Marketing the concept of a solution focused high school is centered around providing educational solutions for students, which community leaders and parents are seeking. The educational needs of the students drive the solution focused concept. So, the very first step to marketing and designing a solution focused alternative high school is to be able to address a pressing educational need for a particular group of students. This is also true if you want to revamp an already existing alternative high school into a school whose program can build solutions, rather than having one or more programs that are disciplinary only in nature and may not offer a rigorous academic curriculum that meet or exceeds standards for an excellent education.

Locate Champions for At-Risk Students

Inevitably, special programs like alternative high schools must have a few champions among their educational leadership. In 1997, Victoria Baldwin, the founding principal of Garza, had no office, no budget, and five months to create and staff an alternative school. Upon first impression, this seems like an impossible task. However, when she began, the superintendent was a big supporter of the high school because at that time there was a critical need to have an alternative high school for dropout prevention due to Austin's escalating dropout rates. In this case, the superintendent was a champion of the school, but in general, it is important to obtain the support of district level administrators as a first step to planning a school program. Connections at the top allow leaders to seek potential funding and much needed community resources. Figuring out who those champions are in the education of at-risk students will be an important starting point to begin a conversation with school leaders and to embark on the journey to develop a solution focused alternative high school.

Timing can be everything when talking to potential champions about the solution focused alternative high school concept or even planting the seeds concerning the idea. It is in those moments when others are in need of a solution—such as when new mandates appear or schools fall short of their targets and face sanctions—that doors may open, and school leaders may be more receptive. Once convinced of the concept, the school leaders are able to navigate funding, the politics of school boards, and community concerns. The founders and the school leaders work hand in hand to advertise this new vision of a solution focused alternative high school to the larger school board and write the mission of the school into policy.

How Much Does It Cost to Educate a Student in a Solution Focused Alternative High School?

The cost of a solution focused alternative high school will be foremost in the mind of many school administrators. The reality is that the cost of educating a student in a solution focused alternative high school is going to be greater than educating a student in a large public high school. But the more important question may be whether or not it is worth the cost? Garza spends over a third more per student than other high schools to operate small classrooms with more counseling and mental health resources. But the long-term benefits to society of graduating high-risk adolescents and sending them to postsecondary education may offset its added expenditures per student. The success of the school and the statistics speak for themselves. Completion rates are above 80% every year, and over 80% enroll in postsecondary education. Test scores of students are consistently at or above the average state scores. For example, the class of 2017 had an average SAT score of Critical Reading: 549 and Math: 522 compared to the state of Texas scores, Critical Reading: 466 and Math: 478.

Securing a place to house a solution focused school may be one of the most significant funding challenges for starting a new alternative high school. The availability of space and the ability to properly equip a school can be costly. Choosing the physical site is an important decision since it represents the ecology of the learning environment and must be given appropriate resources. Alternative schools often are housed in "hand-me-down" buildings, which lack the requirements for creative and innovative educational programs. The need for adequate facilities that meet the educational needs of the students is essential in providing an effective solution focused alternative school as a solution focused climate promotes safety and security among staff and students. This will be a campus where at-risk students will be reintroduced to the opportunities of education. It is important for students to walk into a renovated, technologically up to date, and inviting space. The physical environment will communicate to students that they are deserving of respect and a quality education.

Once again, let's use Garza as an example. It was placed in a 1930s elementary school building, but everything was repainted, updated with appropriate technology, landscaped, outfitted, and decorated to be inviting and motivational to both students and staff. From the very beginning, the philosophy of being both high tech *and* highly student centered guided the physical space and teaching atmosphere of the school. Today, Garza's walls are lined with student art, sculptures, motivational quotes, and inviting colors, all complementing a building renovated with students in mind. The outside is adorned with community gardens and the occasional presence of a miniature horse or other farm animals.

For a student like Eli Cerda, who was a 19-year-old Hispanic male who came to Garza as a dropout, having art on the walls reminded him of what he aspired to become. His large extended family was made up of artists. His father created computer web designs and encouraged Eli to work with art on the computer. Eli had difficulty graduating because of his depression; after his second hospitalization and dropping out of a private charter school, he made his way to Garza. According to Eli, before coming to the solution focused alternative school he had never envisioned a school that valued him and his interest in art. Once at the solution focused high school, Eli finished his courses before his 20th birthday and after graduation planned to combine art and music, perhaps to become a producer. Eli said the solution focused alternative school's environment affected him by, "offering daily reminders of the beautiful art I could create."

How Does the Leadership Work in the Solution Focused Alternative High School?

The composition and functioning of the leadership team in a solution focused alternative high school should be thoughtfully considered. The leadership team at Garza includes a principal, a cabinet of an assistant principal, a student services liaison (most typically the lead school counselor), a college and career counselor, a dropout prevention specialist, and social workers and others that will do outreach in the community. All members of the leadership team work alongside the principal to build solutions for each student; a student cabinet is also advisory to the principal. It is recommended that a solution focused trained professional be part of the initial leadership team of a new alternative high school that wants to become solution focused. It can take time to learn a new language and thought processes when learning the solution focused approach, but it can only get better with practice. Having a specific person dedicated to solution focused training will help the entire team stay true to the solution focused mind-set and can expedite the process if questions can be answered immediately about how new policies and plans fit with the guiding principles of the approach. This solution focused professional will be viewed as a member of the student services support team and could be a counselor, social worker, or another mental health professional.

It is also important that the school's leadership team include a curriculum specialist because the solution focused high school requires that their curriculum be inventive, stimulating, and flexible. One Garza student, Carey, who just turned 18 said, "My old school wasn't the type of school I needed to be in. I don't do things the way everyone else does and I got so far behind." A solution focused alternative high school responds to Carey and to other students with similar academic challenges by creating a self-paced, goal-oriented curriculum allowing students to backload any courses needed and to build foundations that were missed in previous learning experiences. Carey went on to say, "I can now set my own pace and do things on my time and that is why I came. I am allowed to do my work to my best ability and won't be distracted by other teachers and students." Specific approaches to curriculum and instruction are described further in Chapter 6.

First and foremost, the leadership needs to operate as a collaborative team. It is important for leaders to follow the principles of SFBT and to be collaborative while at the same time establishing a clear and consistent set of rules for operation that can be respected and enforced by everyone. The result will be a flexible and collaborative authority structure that will provide both nurturance and accountability in the school system. For student success to occur, everyone needs to be treated with equal care and respect, and their work needs to be supported by the other staff members, while at the same time everyone is held to a high standard for their work. Typical power struggles between teachers and student support team members have to be worked through or else the ultimate goal of student success can be lost. One counselor at Garza said, "The really great thing about being here is that we can do that kind of [solution focused] work in our office and know it will be supported out there by the rest of the school staff."

At-risk students will be super sensitive and emotionally reactive to unresolved conflicts and difficulties between the leaders in the school. Problems in leadership will be quickly transferred into the problems of students. A couple of common mistakes is for leadership to create a too rigid and authoritarian governance structure that impedes communications between leaders and others, causes conflicts to be concealed, and heightens power struggles. This may result in a tense emotional environment, passive aggressive behavior, the challenging of authority, and acting out behavior by at-risk adolescents. A second mistake is to create a permissive governance structure that does not provide enough direction, supervision, and accountability. This results in disorder and out of control behavior from at-risk adolescents. When there is too much permissiveness, leaders and school staff may not have enough influence over students to help educate them or to deal with their daily problems. So, school leadership needs to maintain a flexible balance between setting an agreed upon direction and listening to students for that direction. Above all else, conflict resolutions, harmonious relationships, and united communications are needed from the leaders. This does not mean that conflict will not happen but that these disagreements are resolved in a way that the leadership team comes to an agreement that everyone can honor without working at cross purposes. If leadership works at cross purposes, the at-risk students will be affected, and the students may even unwittingly become involved in these conflicts or will mirror the problems in the leaders and the school system.

Staffing a Solution Focused Alternative School Program

A staff member application for a solution focused alternative high school may not look any different from an application for traditional schools. When conducting interviews, the developers of the solution focused high school are looking for leaders who are willing to fight for students who have faced behavioral health issues, multiple hardships, discrimination, horrific losses, and/or traumatic events. The best teachers often have classroom experience and show they have the flexibility and willingness to learn a new way to understand and teach curricula. The importance of the principal cannot be overemphasized, but it is not so much a matter of personality as it is the commitment to the solution focused approach. The founding principal of Garza is very different in temperament than the current principal, but both are competent solution focused leaders. At Garza, one of the assistant principals said,

> Our teachers really care, but I think one of the reasons we have been successful is because the principal was able to select or choose the same type of people to work for her. If she weren't as dedicated, and if she weren't as friendly or open, then none of us would be.

It is most advantageous when the principal is directly involved in hiring the types of professionals that complement the solution focused approach. One strategy for hiring is to select teachers as aids first, where they gain trust and an understanding of the solution focused mind-set, and later interview for teaching positions as availability opens. When interviewing, the hiring committee should not subscribe to a specific set of interview questions but instead use solution focused questions to gain an understanding of the applicant's teaching philosophy. Questions can be phrased in a way that provides the hiring committee with these sorts of insights; one example might be "How would you respond to a student in this [give a specific challenge] situation?" Exception questions, described in Chapter 1, which are questions that ask people to think about some times when a current problem did not exist or ways that a person may have solved a problem in the past can be asked, along with hypothetical descriptions of problem behaviors that teachers may encounter. For example, "Tell me about a situation where you successfully helped negotiate a student towards success" or "Talk to me about a time when you were successful at discipline in your classroom." Applicants may not have prior knowledge of solution focused interventions, especially when starting a new school, but there are still general attitudes that a staff member can reflect that are evidence they would fit well in an alternative high school. For example, are applicants spending most of the time talking about themselves or about students? When discussing a difficult situation with a student, do they describe what the student was doing wrong or talk about how it was resolved by both the student and themselves? When discussing discipline, are they describing a set of strict rules or a flexible mind-set about consistency and helping students succeed? Ultimately, a solution focused alternative high school must have a team of people who are flexible and motivated toward lifelong learning and who ultimately care about and believe in students.

Training Staff in the Solution Focused Approach

From the very beginning of a solution focused high school, training is crucial and ongoing training should become a standard part of the campus culture as the school develops over time. Two key professionals from the leadership team can play a major part in these trainings: the curriculum specialist and the solution focused specialist. Because Garza has staff that have been immersed in the culture for many years, it does not have an "introductory" training session in solution focused practices. However, with both existing and brand-new alternative schools, an introductory training or orientation is extremely important in order for all staff members to be on the same page.

The original philosophy of Garza's founding principal, Victoria Baldwin, was to train the entire school. It's important to train everyone, so anyone can help students. "Data clerk people were in there, registrars, custodians, because [the principal] said anyone can be an advocate," said one of the administrators. Another teacher said,

> Our custodian is so involved with a lot of our kids and has been a huge advocate and role model. He does citywide basketball and recruits some of our kids for that. He talks with them about manners and accountability; it's just amazing.

Solution focused trainings should be led by experts in SFBT that may come from outside of the school community, educating everyone in the alternative high school on how to have a solution focused conversation. But it is important to quickly develop staff members in the school who can take over the training. Initially, Garza had solution focused experts from the University of Texas at Austin, Steve Hicks School of Social Work and founders of SFBT to conduct the trainings. But each school has to locate their own training resources. In the case of Garza, the initial trainings consisted of consultations with the leadership team, workshops with experts, and classroom coaching. The specific solution focused training approach for Garza has been published in other sources that can be consulted for details on how to conduct the training (see, for example, Franklin & Guz, 2017; Franklin, Montgomery, Baldwin, & Webb, 2012).

Ongoing Professional Development

While introductory trainings are necessary to create a coherent and solution focused mind-set, the most important trainings are the ones that continue throughout the school year. The best way to learn solution focused education is to practice the solution focused mind-set. Practice can be interspersed through staff meetings, often in the form of role-plays presented by administrators or staff members. It takes time and a nonjudgmental space to physically practice challenging cases that may arise. At Garza, practice sessions take place in biweekly meetings in which staff members participate in role-plays of difficult situations that come up with their students. In one example, it had become apparent that students were beginning to linger in the hallways between classes and were showing up late to class. The principal heard this concern from her leadership team and brought it to a staff meeting in the form of a role-play. Teachers acted as both the students and staff members, testing out different ways to respond to students. In acting out both the wrong ways (yelling, "Get your butt to class right this second!") and ways consistent with SFBT (asking the students how they would learn material if they didn't show up on time for class), staff members were able to find their own voice and language in learning how to hold a solution focused conversation with students. The other crucial piece of these role-plays is the nonjudgmental space it provides. A tenured teacher learns just as much as a brand-new counselor by collaborating, listening, and respecting one another during the practice sessions.

Alternative to the more informal role-plays described earlier, a formal workshop should be attended rather than led by the principal so the same individual in charge of being the disciplinarian and boss to staff members isn't also training them. For example, recently, the college and career counselor at Garza gave a workshop on how to respond to students when questions about college came up in the classroom. The staff were able to learn some collaborative and useful ways to respond to a student who stated no interest in college. The principle attended this workshop and by taking on the role of a leaner, modeled professional development for the rest of the staff. They learn to ask solution focused questions, such as "Has there ever been a time that you thought about going to college?" and "Who in the past has encouraged you to go to college?" These questions replace less useful authoritarian responses, such as, "Well, it's a requirement so you have to meet with the counselor now."

Which Students Attend a Solution Focused Alternative High School Program?

The typical alternative high school enrolls students who are at risk for various reasons. To hold the alternative status, Garza, for example, must have 75% of students fall into an "at-risk" category (e.g., low income, pregnant, homeless, underrepresented status). Most educators are familiar with the at-risk categories, but the labels and statistics do not do justice to the actual life stories of students and the range of issues these students present.

One Garza student who left her former school because of her pregnancy said in a research interview,

> I quit going to school like in February of last year. I did not go March, April, or May. I had just gotten pregnant and I didn't go to school very much; I just didn't. I just didn't feel like going. I knew that wasn't the end of it. I knew I was going to graduate. It just wasn't going to happen at that moment.

Other Garza students talk about substance use and mental health challenges in themselves and family members. One student stated,

> I would go to class high almost every day—on marijuana. There was a lot of coke dealing at my old high school and I did do it in the restroom a couple of times. I smoked weed every day.

Another student talked about how her mom's drinking affected her life: "When she and my dad broke up when I was eight or nine, she started drinking and dating guys. Some of them hit her and some of them were crazy." Another student spoke about her overdose:

> I didn't knowingly attempt to do suicide but I did overdose and the ambulance came and got me. My mom found me in the bathroom and I was unconscious. I was rushed to the E.R. and they put charcoal down in my system and got rid of all the drugs or whatever. I was an inpatient at a hospital during my sophomore year.

Yet another student spoke about her family problems that involved substance use:

> Well, my dad has a real bad alcohol problem and he's a very serious alcoholic. My mom smokes marijuana on a pretty regular basis. That's made things real difficult because my dad drinks and doesn't like smoking, my mom smokes and doesn't like drinking. Me, my brother, and Joe [friend] are all on the same page as far as partying goes, I mean I was never into anything more than smoking weed. Because my mom was on that page with us, my dad was kind of an outcast. We've just been fighting for the past three years to try and get it to a level where everybody is pleased with the situation and it's just been rough.

Finally, a student who graduated from Garza provides a vivid example of how her relationship with her mother interfered with her schooling:

> She [the student's mother] told me to pack up everything I would need and never come back. So, I packed a bag. I was crying the whole time. So, I went outside and called my ex-boyfriend again and he came to pick me up. And I was waiting outside when she came running outside with a machete in her hand. I mean she was off the edge. She took my bag away from me. I was screaming. This was like four o'clock in the morning by now. I'm outside screaming my head off. The woman's out here with knives. I was really freaking out. And my boyfriend shows up and managed to calm her down some and she eventually let us go. I knew I couldn't stay in the house with her. So, I was gone and kind of stayed at various people's houses for several days. Eventually she called and asked me to come home and we worked it out as we usually do. Those horrible emotions stay inside me and just, you know, rot. I have incidents like that with my mom a lot.

How Are Students Selected for the Solution Focused Alternative School?

Alternative school students like the ones described earlier should not be forced to attend a solution focused alternative high school because it goes against everything the school stands for. Instead, the school is to be a school of choice. Students are granted the decision-making process that allows them to make the choice and to say, "I like this program. I want to be here." Students interview for admission and earn a spot. This results in the perception that every student who is at a solution focused high school is there because it was their choice, and they were accepted.

One student said in a research interview that she chose to come to Garza because she wanted a different environment for her learning:

> I can't come and go as I please, but people are real understanding. I learn more, because I learn it on my own. I actually have to do something. It's hard, but it's not given to me like it is at other schools. You know, the curriculum is just given to you at regular schools. You fill out some worksheets and that's it. You don't learn anything. Here you have to do research. You have to figure it out on your own. You get help, but they're not going to give you things.

When seeking out students who may be a good fit for a new solution focused alternative high school, word is spread, and the self-paced approach for students who are at risk of dropping out is advertised through the school district's counselors and administrators. This may not look like a typical advertisement by way of poster or press release but is instead a simple conversation held between students, their parents (if applicable), and counselors, who explain that another option for degree completion exists. We recommend that typical printed advertisements be avoided in order to prevent "us" versus "them" stigmas for a student entering a counselor's office. Instead, a description of the school is verbally provided to the student by a counselor or teacher, and then the student makes a choice to interview at this new alternative high school.

Once a student is interested in the possibility of attending the solution focused school, the student comes in for an interview with the principal. A conversation is held before the official interviewing begins, with the principal explaining that the interview is a two-way street. This means that the principal is interviewing the student, and the student is interviewing the principal. During the interview, the student is directed to ask, "Is this school a good fit for me?" At the same time, the administrator considers whether or not the student is a good fit for the school. As mentioned before, the emphasis is also placed on the choice of the student: Does the student *want* to be here? Without that choice, the school becomes a disciplinary center where students are sent rather than a choice the student has made to be a part of a new educational opportunity that will build solutions. During the actual interview, questions are asked of the student, such as "What worked at your old high school?" "What didn't work?" and "How can our school fit your needs?"

The principal will also explain the solution-building approach, how the school focuses on the future, and that the student can start there with a clean slate, perhaps even stating, "Whatever happened in your past education is the past, and you can choose to become a new person here." Additionally, the principal emphasizes to the prospective student the school's high standards and expectations of respect towards all individuals. In the same mind-set of holding high standards for staff members, students are expected to raise themselves to a higher standard. Garza has a code of honor that communicates these expectations. The Garza Code of Honor, states that everyone:

- demonstrate personal honor and integrity at all times,
- choose peace over conflict, and
- [provide] respect for ourselves and others.

The principal will verbally ask for a commitment from a potential student to this honor code, saying, "I am going to treat you with respect and in turn I expect you to treat me with respect. What do you think about what I am saying?" The principal will additionally explain that if the student is experiencing some barrier in reaching those higher standards, the student support team will help the student build solutions to achieve educational goals.

The student is encouraged to be very honest during this interview, as there are no right or wrong answers to the questions. Consistent with the solution focused mind-set, the principal is looking for reasons to grant the student acceptance into the school, not reasons to deny the individual. Instead of looking for students to respond in the right way, an administrator will be thinking about whether or not the school is equipped to fully support the student to reach a goal of graduation. Can this student's life provide space for success in this school right now? Students with specific struggles, such as homelessness, would require a detailed plan on how the school can best support them, which might include connections with the students' shelter caseworker and a plan for meals. The administrator must consider if the school's student support team has the appropriate resources to best help this student. If they do, the student becomes part of the student body.

Student Orientation

A student orientation is set once the student and principal agree that the solution focused alternative school is a good fit, and the student says yes to an opportunity to attend the school. Just as staff members must be oriented to this new solution focused mind-set, students also need to attend an orientation to help them adjust to this new language of solutions in education, a self-paced model, and a new school environment. An orientation covers typical logistics of students entering a new school: information about the school and its purpose, an individual meeting with the student's counselor to explain fully what credits are needed for graduation and when it could be achieved, receipt and comprehension of the academic schedule, and a tour of the school. Students are also asked to do some reflections and goal setting about their future while in orientation. Future-oriented and miracle questions and goal setting from SFBT are often used to guide these reflections. A miracle question, as described in Chapter 1, for example, asks students to imagine the future when problems are solved and helps a student express what they want (goals), paying attention to small details in what the student will be doing differently when the problems are better or no longer present. It may also incorporate relationship questions to help a student further think about the responses of others in relation to what they do. For example, a student may be asked to imagine that a miracle has occurred, and their educational problems are better, what will they be doing differently or ask them to move themselves forward in time and talk about what they will be doing after graduation? They may be further asked about who will be proud of them or how others will react to these accomplishments? Solution focused questions, such as the miracle and relationship questions, are more than asking a student to use their imagination because the questions tap into a student's aspirations and orients them to practice thinking about goals and solutions.

It is surprising to some educators that the student orientation does not include training about the solution focused approach. Instead, the solution-building concept is introduced to new students through experiences during the interview and orientation process, and is further demonstrated while attending the alternative high school, which continuously models how solution focused questions and language are used. Solution talk becomes evident to students through their conversations with staff and also by observing how staff talk to one another. Following the "anytime entrance" and "anytime exit" structure of a self-paced model, a new school would potentially host a larger orientation for all students, then transition into hosting these orientations every two weeks as they begin building the student body.

Professional Development Sustains the School's Practices: An Example

Garza's principal was sitting in the back of the room at a staff development meeting while a professor from the University of Texas at Austin did a presentation on the use of SFBT in schools. The presentation included role-plays and practical knowledge that the staff could utilize in their classrooms. Garza had recently hired several new teachers and had an influx of students with suicidality and mental health challenges. The combination made the principal think that it was time for a refresher from an expert on SFBT.

One of the newer teachers was in the front of the room listening intently. Mr. Guzman had several students in his classroom who engaged in self-harm and who had been diagnosed with bipolar disorder or depression. Although these students were receiving counseling at Garza as well as in the community, Mr. Guzman wanted to be able to support these students in the classroom. For Mr. Guzman, this was not the first time he had students in his class who self-harmed or had other mental health issues. In his previous position at another high school, it was fairly common to see students with fresh cuts on their arm and legs. In these cases, Mr. Guzman would make a referral to the school counselor, but since the school was so large and understaffed, Mr. Guzman never received a follow up on a student's status. Additionally, Mr. Guzman felt underprepared to help these students in the classroom.

During the training, Mr. Guzman and the other staff role-played and practiced solution focused techniques. After the training, Dr. Webb asked Mr. Guzman how he felt about the training.

"I am so glad we had this training!" said Mr. Guzman. "The students at Garza are intense and I want to be able to support them in the classroom and this training makes me believe I can."

Dr. Webb smiled and said, "I am glad to hear that. We want to support both our staff and our students. It takes a community to help these students succeed."

Following the training, Mr. Guzman was able to have conversations with students he considered to be most at risk and made several referrals to the student services team (a group of faculty tasked with following up on difficult cases), the counselors, and the Communities In Schools' social workers. For all the referrals, Mr. Guzman found the process to be direct, easy, and helpful. He received follow up from both the student services team and the counselors and social workers. In fact, one of the social workers came into his classroom to help with a student who was crying and appeared to be thinking about killing herself. Rather than a teacher who was ill-equipped to help his students, Mr. Guzman was beginning to feel like a team member not just in the students' education but in their mental health interventions as well.

Key Points to Keep in Mind

- To be ready to develop a solution focused alternative high school for high-risk adolescents, school leaders have to understand and embrace a solution focused mind-set and fully implement the solution focused approach.

- Trust, respect, and cooperation between everyone in the alternative high school helps create a cohesive campus community; these are requisite conditions for the education of high-risk adolescents.
- Everyone in the solution focused school must be trained and supported continuously to use the solution focused approach.
- The solution focused alternative high school is an educational support program to other high schools and must be an independent high school that is valued by educational leadership throughout a community.
- It will cost more to educate students in a solution focused alternative high school, but the educational results and benefit to society are worth it.
- Administrators hired must be dedicated to the solution focused approach and have a desire to create a campus community support team that involves everyone.
- Teachers hired must have a true commitment to the students' success above all other qualities, along with the ability to be flexible in learning new curriculum.
- Students must always have the choice to attend the solution focused school, demonstrated through an interview process where the student can ask "Is this school a good fit for me?" and the principal can ask "Can we support this student in the best way possible?"

Summary

This chapter describes how to develop a solution focused alternative high school. A solution focused mind-set and training in SFBT by the entire campus community is necessary to start and sustain the school. People and their relationships are also central to a successful solution focused school including administrators, teachers, students, parents, community partners, and mental health professionals. A culture of trust, respect, and solution-building conversations are essential to the daily interactions within the school; these interpersonal characteristics are fundamental to the successful education of high-risk adolescents. This chapter provides a big picture overview, addressing issues such as gaining school district and community support, establishing a leadership team, securing funding and staffing, selecting students, orienting selected students to the school program, and conducting solution focused training. Even though, this chapter has been written from the vantage point of creating a solution focused high school from scratch, the contents of this chapter are believed to also be useful to transforming existing alternative education programs into high schools that follow solution focused principles.

Note

1 Cases presented in this chapter are taken from research interviews of students that attend an alternative high school and staff experiences working with these students. Names and some information have been changed to protect the confidentiality of the students involved. Some of these interviews were made possible by the generous support of the Hogg Foundation for Mental Health at The University of Texas at Austin.

References

Franklin, C., & Guz, S. (2017). Tier 1 approach: Schools adopting SFBT model. In J. S. Kim, M. S. Kelly, & C. Franklin (Eds.), *Solution-focused brief therapy in schools: A 360-degree view of research and practice principles* (2nd ed.). New York, NY: Oxford University Press.

Franklin, C., Hopson, L., & Dupper, D. (2013). Guides for designing alternative schools for dropout prevention. In C. Franklin, M. B. Harris, & P. A. Allen-Meares (Eds.), *The school services sourcebook, second edition* (pp. 405–418). New York, NY: Oxford University Press.

Franklin, C., Montgomery, K., Baldwin, V., & Webb, L. (2012). Research and development of a solution-focused high school. In C. Franklin, T. Trepper, W. Gingerich, & E. McCullum (Eds.), *Solution-focused brief therapy: A handbook of evidence based practice* (pp. 371–389). New York, NY: Oxford University Press.

3

How to Build Cooperative, Solution Focused Relationships

A Story to Get Started

Seth[1] came to Gonzalo Garza Independence High School in the middle of the fall semester. At his former school, he was frequently suspended and rarely completed homework. At home, he was equally difficult. He was verbally combative with his mother and younger brother, and would threaten physical violence. Seth's mother was a single, low-income woman who was completely overwhelmed by him. As a result, Seth received little supervision and guidance at home.

When Seth came into Garza, his appearance was striking. He was tall and had a sturdy build. He did not brush his teeth, shower, or use deodorant, and as a result, he had a strong smell of body odor. His voice was soft, but his tone was consciously dismissive. It was quickly apparent to the staff that building a relationship with Seth would take some work since he made a point of not being likeable and isolating himself from people. However, student-staff rapport is at the center of building a cooperative relationship in a solution focused alternative school, and this is essential for solution-building.

When Seth began classes, he found himself drawn to computer science. When he walked into the computer science classroom, he immediately gravitated to the row of shiny, bright desks. Since he came from a low-income household, computers, especially state-of-the-art desktops, were new to him. Before class had officially begun, Seth had logged onto the computer and was playing with the desktop settings. Ms. Amari, the teacher in the classroom, noticed his strong interest and introduced herself to him. Seth looked over at Ms. Amari and quietly said, "Hello."

Ms. Amari smiled and began class. She noticed that Seth easily followed instructions and could do a lot of the work on his own. When it was time to change classrooms, he was so absorbed in the computer that he was unaware of the time. Ms. Amari prompted him to leave but said, "If you'd like to come back during lunch, you are welcome to do so; you just can't eat or drink by the computers."

When it was time for lunch, Seth came back into Ms. Amari's classroom and asked if he could be on the computers.

"Of course, Seth," said Ms. Amari. "I'll be here if you want some instruction."

Over several weeks, Seth built a cooperative relationship with Ms. Amari and friendships with a few other students who also came into the computer lab during lunch. Although he remained quiet in his other classrooms and mainly kept to himself outside his group of friends, his loner demeanor dropped, which gave him room to gain a new reputation of being kind, responsible, and smart. This was the first time Seth had gained a positive reputation at school; this was also the first time he felt like he had teachers who liked him. In turn, he came to know the teachers as patient and consistent people. The cooperative and positive relationships he built at the solution focused alternative high school paved the road to his graduation. After two and half years at the school, Seth graduated and enrolled at a four-year university to further explore his interest in computer science.

Introduction

Most school social workers, counselors, and educators know that relationships are critical to student engagement, academic achievement, and dropout prevention. The change strategies of Solution Focused Brief Therapy (SFBT) have been successfully used in schools with students from diverse cultural backgrounds (Franklin & Montgomery, 2014) and are useful in building cooperative relationships with high-risk adolescents, even when they are reluctant to receive help (DeJong & Berg, 2012; Franklin & Hopson, 2009). Rapport with students is the active ingredient in all academic, emotional, and developmental progress in a school setting. In order for students to set and meet their own goals, they must build relationships with the staff, who help them navigate goal setting and progress. Often, at-risk students have experienced trauma, poor attachment, and environmental distress. For school staff, facing large developmental and systematic barriers can be overwhelming. SFBT techniques can help teachers and other staff purposefully build rapport with these students and help them in achieving their goals.

The aim of this chapter is to show how cooperative relationships between students and teachers can have a reverberating impact so that positive relationships lead to better outcomes in the classroom. This chapter describes how relationships are built, enhanced, and maintained using SFBT. Solution focused relationship-building techniques include being student centered, strengths based, and present and future oriented. Furthermore, these techniques allow students to define their own goals and measure their own progress. Stories and personal experiences are used to enhance the content of this chapter and to show how SFBT is used to build relationships between teachers and students.

Building Relationships

School teachers and other staff are oftentimes reminded that relationships with students are the most important part of classroom instruction. However, rarely is there any practical advice or techniques given on how to build these relationships. One Garza teacher noted,

> I used to hear 'build relationships!' over and over again with no understanding of what that meant. I thought I was supposed to just naturally do that. Now I know that counselors and social workers are taught to do that and that rapport building is a skill I can work on building. SFBT helped me understand how to build relationships with students. Now I have techniques I can use and rely on that work with different student populations.

It is normal to feel confused or lost at the thought of building relationships with a variety of students. Teachers, administrators, and specialized instructional support staff are all individuals with their own unique backgrounds. An individual's background (race, gender, ethnicity, nationality, sexual orientation, class, etc.) creates a perception of what relationship building looks like. For example, people from different cultures and genders often have unique ways of relating to people. In America, most helping professionals are white women who have a specific way of communicating with others in personal and professional settings (Ryde, 2009). It is natural to have a background and a personal way of relating to other people; however, it is also important to recognize that not all students and staff come from the same place. Therefore, it is essential that teachers and school staff are able to build relationships and serve students who come from a wide variety of backgrounds.

In a solution focused setting, the student's perceptions, definitions, and goals are at the center of the relationship. By using a student-centered approach to relationship building, school staff ensures that personal values, judgments, and expectations are not being pushed onto the students. The relationship-building techniques outlined in this chapter are effective with all populations of students as they follow core tenants of SFBT:

- Be student centered.
- Be strengths based.
- Be present and future oriented.
- Allow students to create goals for themselves.
- Allow students to measure their own progress.
- Reinforce student success and amplify student progress.

As a Garza teacher noted, using solution focused techniques to create relationships helps professionals feel more confident:

> I am a White woman teaching at a solution focused alternative school. We have a lot of different students on our campus and I was finding myself unable to build rapport easily with the underserved students, especially Black male students. Our Black male students were not graduating as easily or as quickly as our White students. I did not understand what they needed from me. After learning about the strengths-based approach and solution focused techniques I am much more able to serve the Black male student population. Before I was setting expectations for them; now I know they need to set goals for themselves. They define who they are and what they want from their education, not me.

Solution Focused Techniques to Help Foster Relationships with Students

How to Be Student Centered

In this quote from a Garza teacher, we see how rapport-building skills can be developed by using solution focused techniques. In a solution focused school, relationships are *student centered*, meaning that the relationship is oriented around the student's needs. Although this sounds simple and obvious in thought, it takes more conscious effort to implement. For example, being student centered requires patience and consistency.

In building student relationships, it is important to remember that the relationship is ultimately about the student. When rapport is taking a long time to build, it is easy to get frustrated and feel rejected. Even seasoned adult teachers and staff can get hurt feelings or form a grudge against a student that is difficult. This is natural. It is important, however, to identify these feelings and set them aside. This is done through two steps: (1) regaining perspective and (2) self-care. When feelings of rejection or hurt bubble up, solution focused teachers have cited these two things as being helpful. One teacher stated,

> I've been teaching for a decade and a half and I still get hurt feelings when a student is more difficult to build a relationship with. When they ignore me or brush me off, it hurts. I came into teaching because I care so naturally, I'm vulnerable to such feelings. However, I am a professional and an adult. These are teenagers, teenagers who have experienced loss and trauma. For them, attachment is hard and I have to be conscious of where they are coming from. I meet them where they are rather than expecting them to come to me. Additionally, I take care of myself outside of work. They don't teach you that in school, but I need it. These students are not my family or my kids. When I take care of me, I am better at work and it's easier for me to readjust my perspective when things get difficult.

This quote gets at the core of being student centered: *Meet the students where they are*. Rather than being angry with students for not building the relationship you want from them, take a step back and remember your role. For example, teachers may like it when students voluntarily talk to them in the hall or come visit before school starts. However, not all students are able to build that type of relationship. If a student has difficult circumstances at home or is struggling in some way, forming relationships may be a challenge. If this means a student comes to class and rarely speaks to the teacher, that is fine! The silver lining is that the student is coming to class. Meeting students where they are means being patient and consistent with students and accepting what they are able to do in the present moment.

In order to have conversations about change, a strong relationship between the teacher and student is important. A series of positive interactions between a teacher and a student establishes a foundation of trust and rapport required to have conversations about change and goals. For many of the students at a solution focused alternative high school, building rapport and healthy attachments with adults is difficult. The ability to create appropriate, healthy, and meaningful relationships is not a skill people come out of the womb knowing; it is something we are taught. Many individuals from healthy families and caring guardians learn it at home. These skills are then reinforced in school, and students expand their skills and even their individual strengths.

But for students at an alternative high school, it is likely that rapport-building skills were never learned at home or reinforced at school. If they were taught at all, they were likely disrupted by trauma, mental illness, or substance use. The solution focused school setting may be the first time a youth experienced a positive interaction with an adult or teacher. It is essential that teachers and school staff identify a student's experience and be purposeful in their own responses. By acknowledging the vulnerability required on the part of students to have conversations about goals and change, we can begin meeting them where they are.

One Garza teacher discussed how in her classroom, she met a student where he was. She said,

> We have a student who is very quiet and withdrawn. He usually has his head down. As I do my rounds I tap on his shoulder and he usually pops his head up and gets to work. One day the student did not pop his head up when I tapped him on his shoulder. I asked him how he was doing and he responded that he lost his motivation to work. I inquired what was going on. He said he got lunch detention. The student's *real* [emphasis added] concern was not being able to get fresh air and that he looks forward to the fresh air since he is not a senior and therefore not allowed to leave campus during lunch. The student continued to

> express his frustration about other concerns and I listened. Afterwards, he was able to get some work accomplished. I was glad I had previously started to form a relationship with the student so he was able to talk about his concerns and then be productive in the classroom and get his work done.

How to Be Strengths Based

Another core tenant of solution focused relationship building is being strengths based. To be strengths based means to actively identify positive things about a student. For the student that is nonverbal with a teacher but comes to class, a pessimistic viewpoint might be "Geez, the student never participates and looks so bored!" In contrast, a strengths-based perspective is "Wow! That student never misses class. He does his work and is never late." It may seem obvious but consider how much more difficult the student's case would be if the individual never came to class?

The strengths-based approach places priority on the authentic relationship the teacher has with students and does not use a punitive model of punishment to make progress with them. This is a difference that students recognize at a solution focused alternative school. "I notice that the teachers here notice my good qualities more," said one Garza student.

> They don't try to scare me into learning math; I'm not made to feel stupid for not understanding something. I like [that] I can learn things because I feel respected here. It never feels like it's a do it or fail situation.

As this student notes, a strengths-based approach is a non-shaming approach. It makes room for some mistakes along the way. Often, a student will take several steps forward and one step back. A student may even stagnate for a period of time. In the strengths-based method of relationship building, the teacher relies on the authentic belief that students make progress, even when it does not look like it.

Using the Students' Language

When creating positive relationships with students, it is important to use their language. This does not mean slang or pop culture references. Rather, use their language when it comes to their growth. In Chapter 1, there was a section on scaling questions. Scaling questions are used to gauge where the student perceives growth to be happening. For example, on a scale of 1–10, a student may put a goal of finishing science credits at an 8. For this student, an 8 could mean "need to finish two more assignments to complete high school science" or it could mean "finally completed my first project in a science credit." For these reasons, scaling questions are an opportunity to support students and help them work toward their goal.

When a student rates a science goal at a 7 (out of 10), it means that individual is proud and happy with what has been achieved. This is an opportunity to compliment the progress and amplify a student's feelings of pride. A teacher might say "I am so glad that you placed yourself at a 7. You have worked hard and have gained a lot of ground recently." However, if the placement is a 3, this is an indicator that the student is discontent with his or her learning progress. For teachers, this is an opportunity to ask, "So what would take you from a 3 to a 4?" or "Why are you at a 3 rather than a 2?" As the student addresses these questions or begins to define what gains would stir feelings of progress, it is important for the teacher to listen to the language used to describe goals.

Students may use a variety of languages to talk about themselves. Often the language students use is reflective of their background and identities. This is why solution focused techniques work with a variety of students. The 1–10 scale is a numeric scale that is used to anchor and gage progress with no absolute meaning until the student assigns meaning to it. The definition of the student's progress or future steps comes from the student, not the teacher. The language the student uses to talk about hopes is incredibly important and helps staff reopen a conversation about goals in the future.

At a solution focused high school, teachers meet with students weekly to define goals and check on progress. Students are not always eager to reopen conversations about their learning goals, so teachers use the students' language to help reengage the student. Here is an example of such a conversation:

Teacher: "I wanted to point out to you this week that at the beginning of semester, four weeks ago, you said you were at a 10 because you would not have to finish high school in a GED course. You said you felt strongly about finishing high school on a campus with students your age."

Student: "Did I really say that?"

Teacher: "You did. Do you want to see the goal sheet from your first week here?"

Student: "Yeah."

Teacher: "Here you go!"

Student: "Wow... I just wanted to begin coming to class. Now I want to finish my science credits"

Teacher: "What's it feel like looking at this now?"

Student: "It reminds me of why I'm here, I guess."

Teacher: "I can imagine that it would. Now that we have looked at where you were, let's take a look at where you are now."

Student: "Sure."

In this example, the teacher used goals from the student's first week at the solution focused alternative school to reengage the student in the conversation. Notice how the teacher did not need to convince the student that the conversation was important or intimidate the student into talking about goals. The teacher engaged the student by being student centered and mirroring the language the student uses.

Listening and Co-Constructing Meanings

The role of a school staff member in students' change processes involves listening to the students and co-constructing meanings from the students' conversations. This process of purposefully listening to and reflecting back key words that are change related and strengths oriented was discussed in Chapter 1. Recall from that chapter, the solution focused techniques of Listen, Select, and Build. More simply put, this means listening for strengths and solutions when students talk and being curious about what is being said by asking questions and purposefully amplifying the students' progress and change. Another example for how co-construction of meaning works in conversations and facilitates rapport and meaningful change may be useful. Take, for example, this conversation between a teacher and a student about the student's repeated tardiness to school.

Student: "I have been trying harder to get to school on time but I have to work late and I just can't get here. I work at Taco Bell. I usually have to close down and I don't get out of work until almost 2:00. That is why I skip first period. I am just too tired to come that early. I can't stop work because I have to pay my bills. I don't have anybody to help me with money and I never get any sleep. I am just too tired to wake-up."

Teacher: "That must be really hard for you to close down and never getting any sleep and I can see why you have a hard time coming to first period, being so tired. You mentioned working harder to get here on time?"

In this part of the conversation, the teacher purposefully listens to what the student has to say and acknowledges the student's point of view and further purposefully *selects* the words that indicate some kind of change in the preferred direction toward coming to school on time.

Student: "Yea, I actually set two alarms today and that is why I was only late to first period instead of skipping it."

Teacher: "Yes, I noticed you were here earlier today. So, it sounds like you want to be on time."

Student: "Yes, I want to get here on time. I need this class to graduate."

Teacher: "So, this is important for you to get to school on time. You want to graduate!"

Student: "Yea, I am just so tired."

Teacher: "Of course, you are tired but it also sounds like you are willing to try hard and you were able to get here earlier today. I know you have come to first period on time in the past. What did you do to get here on time on those days?"

In this part of the conversation, the teacher and student *build* on the preferred direction toward getting to school on time by discussing the student's goal to complete the first period class and graduate. The teacher follows up with an exception question aimed at continuing to *build* a solution.

As was illustrated, through conversing with and listening to the student, both the student and teacher can gain perspective on a problem and together identify a workable solution. Oftentimes, assumptions are made about how students learn or what students are challenged by; however, a solution cannot be found until both parties understand the student's vision of the goal. Asking students to clarify what they want for themselves provides students with the opportunity to explore and vocalize their goals. These opportunities to talk about oneself do not often occur in day to day conversations and are therefore a sacred part of building rapport with students.

In another example, a Garza teacher talked about how she used listening and co-constructing as tools for change:

> I have a student who, for a period, seemed to be allowing bouts of emotion to interrupt her academic progress on a near-daily basis. She would get upset and/or begin crying and, often, leave early. Reasonably often, when other options didn't seem viable, I would sit with her and listen until she stopped crying or being angry. This worked but also seemed odd to me because that is not my role. I am not a counselor; my focus is academics, so I kept wondering how I could reconstruct the conversation toward academics. After some exploring I did seem to find, via the application of what I might term a 'modified' version of the exception question, a potentially workable method for mitigation: 'When have you written about your feelings?' For some backstory, the student is nearly always highly receptive to, even eager for, writing challenges—perhaps more so than any other student I've encountered. Almost invariably, if the student is stuck or needs an idea, a mere seed or spark or suggestion, however casual, will set off an eye-blaze and a flurry of clattering computer keys. Knowing this, when the student was upset and I perhaps didn't have the time to sit and give the student the full spectrum of attention and emotional support [she needed], I suggested that the student write how she was feeling. The student nodded, and was off. The writing wasn't necessarily class related, but it did seem to refocus or change the energy toward academics.

In this example, the teacher integrated the student's desire to express her feelings with the student's willingness to write. Rather than sitting down and talking with the student when the teacher did not have the time to do so, the teacher used the student's strengths and her own solution, which were discovered by listening to the student, to co-create a task for the student that led to a more preferable way of managing her emotions in the classroom.

The Nonlinear Process of Change

Change is not linear and is not always a smooth journey. This nonlinear process may be frustrating for students and teachers. It is natural for teachers to be excited about student successes and feel discouraged when they do not meet expectations. During these difficult periods, it is important that teachers rely on their professional training and take care of themselves outside of work. For example, one Garza teacher noted that in a period of difficultly with a student, she reoriented the relationship with compliments and emotional support:

> I work on giving positive feedback whenever possible. This was not as easy as one would believe it to be. Yes, it is easy to give positive feedback for positive actions but not everything a student does is positive. This was an interesting challenge that I did not expect. For the most part our students' actions are positive.

There may be a period of time when the student does not seem engaged or motivated toward progress. This is when patience and the strengths-based approach are essential. If a student is coming to class but barely turning in assignments, it is important to focus on attendance in class. If teenagers want to skip class, they're more than capable of doing so. However, when a student comes to class it is a sign that something is gained from attending that particular class and from being in school. In these situations, it is important to identity what students are getting from class and amplify it.

An Example of What Building Relationships Can Do

Jason came into class looking distraught. He was distracted, mopey, and clearly not in the mood to work. Usually his teacher would try to redirect him from his distractions right away, but today, since Mr. Chopra had some information about what Jason was struggling with outside of class, he relented a little. Instead, Mr. Chopra tried something else.

"Jason you have that poem assignment due today," he said. "You seem upset, though, and distracted. I'm going to give you some time to get situated while I help the other students get started, and then I'm going to sit with you."

Mr. Chopra received an inaudible response from Jason that more or less meant he agreed. About 10 minutes later, Mr. Chopra sat next to Jason to check in on him.

Instead of trying to get Jason started immediately on the assignment, Mr. Chopra invited him to share his feelings and frustrations.

"What's being in class like for you right now?" he asked.

Mr. Chopra was surprised when Jason began talking about his frustrations and feelings. He discussed what was going on outside of school, including his unstable living situation and the domestic violence he witnessed at home. Then Jason began to connect how his life frustrations magnified his frustrations in the classroom. On his own, he continued to identify what the problem with the assignment was and wondered if he had a learning disability or "something."

Mr. Chopra saw that Jason was not feeling motivated to work toward his goals at the moment, so he asked Jason to search for exceptions.

"I'm hearing that you are frustrated with school right now," he said. "When do you feel good about your school work?"

The answers to the exception question arose naturally from Jason and revealed Jason's own perspective of himself.

"I feel good when I check something off," said Jason. "Like when I complete an assignment or a credit. The in between when I don't feel like I am accomplishing is where I get down." He also remembered a time when he didn't have this difficulty. "I like to read, but I have trouble writing about what I am reading in the papers assigned."

These statements reflected Jason's learning gaps. Later, Mr. Chopra noted,

> There seems to be a block when it comes to writing. He has a strong grasp of grammar, a modest vocabulary, a strong understanding of what he needs to do, but becomes extremely anxious and frustrated when asked to write something down that is more than a response to a simple question with a specific answer. He said he did not have this problem with the assignments in math and science. Particularly math, because in math there's a right answer. There's a formula to follow that guides you and you know what to do.

Suddenly, Mr. Chopra felt an overwhelming sense of excitement: This was the aha moment! Previously, Mr. Chopra had been trying to encourage Jason by telling him that he did not need to worry about what he wrote but just "give it a shot." However, now Mr. Chopra was seeing that the "just go for it!" statement overwhelmed Jason because he did not know where to begin.

Mr. Chopra began to look for a solution to offer Jason. Later, he stated: "I think that [open-ended assignments] increases his frustration because it's too ambiguous, and it doesn't solve his problem. He wants a guide."

Mr. Chopra asked Jason if it would help if he gave him a template for the poem he should write, with guidelines similar to a formula. Jason said yes, he'd be open to trying it. Mr. Chopra printed out a handout that he was familiar with and walked Jason through the instructions and an example. After the instruction was over Jason immediately began writing his poem using the guidelines.

At the end of class, Jason was not completely finished with the poem, but he had written more in the last 5–10 minutes of class than Mr. Chopra had seen him write in a long time. Jason stumbled on a solution without really knowing it and gave Mr. Chopra an opportunity to meet him where he was academically. The conversation was valuable on many levels. Mr. Chopra learned from Jason's perspective about what was going on in his life and also gained insight into Jason's thought processes and frustrations about the assignment as well as English class in general. Finally, Mr. Chopra not only watched Jason come to his own solution, but he also watched him articulate the problem clearly and advocate for himself.

Key Points to Keep in Mind

- Student-teacher relationships are the active ingredient in any change; this includes academic, emotional, and development growth.
- Rapport building is a skill that can be built upon; solution focused techniques can assist teachers in advancing this skill.
- Solution focused relationship-building techniques include being student centered, being strengths based, being present and future oriented, allowing students to define their own goals, and allowing students to measure their own progress.
- Being student centered means meeting the students where they are rather than expecting them to fulfill teacher expectations of what a relationship should look like.
- A strengths-based approach requires actively and consciously identifying strengths in students.
- Listening to students' use of language regarding their goals and progress is a good way to reopen the conversation about goals later on. Scaling questions can be especially helpful in mirroring students' language.
- Student growth is not linear. Growth will typically move three steps forward, two steps back, and occasionally even a step to the side.

Summary

In order for students to make progress, a strong student-teacher relationship needs to form. This chapter explores the importance of rapport building, an essential part of a solution focused alternative school and a skill that can be developed. Solution focused relationship-building techniques work with a variety of student populations. These techniques are beneficial to students but are also helpful to teachers and all staff who begin to experience stress or feelings of rejection from students. This chapter discusses that while using these techniques, it is important to remember to keep the work centered on the student and to also keep it strengths based. Additionally, it reminds readers that progress is not linear; there are many steps forward and back. It is essential to be patient and consistent in the relationship with a student and to keep working toward the student's goals.

Note

1 Cases presented in this chapter are taken from research interviews of students that attend an alternative high school and staff experiences working with these students. Names and some information have been changed to protect the confidentiality of the students involved. Some of these interviews were made possible by the generous support of the Hogg Foundation for Mental Health at The University of Texas at Austin.

References

DeJong, P., & Berg, I. K. (2012). *Interviewing for solutions*. Belmont, CA: Cengage Learning.

Franklin, C., & Hopson, L. (2009). Involuntary clients in public schools: Solution-focused interventions. In R. Rooney (Ed.), *Strategies for work with involuntary clients* (2nd ed., pp. 322–333). New York, NY: Columbia University Press.

Franklin, C., & Montgomery, K. (2014). Does solution-focused brief therapy work? In J. S. Kim, *Solution-focused brief therapy: A multicultural approach* (pp. 32–54). Thousand Oaks, CA: Sage Publications.

Ryde, J. (2009). *Being white in the helping professions: Developing effective intercultural awareness*. London, UK: Jessica Kingsley Publishers.

4 Creating Goals, Positive Expectancies, and Positive Emotions for Success

A Story to Get Started

Ms. Martinez[1] worked in several public schools within the local school district before she accepted a job at the solution focused alternative high school Gonzalo Garza Independence High School. Prior to joining Garza, Ms. Martinez loved teaching but found it difficult to work with several of her students because she felt unprepared to help them deal with their problems outside of school. She wondered, "How do I help a child who is homeless or who is in the foster care system? How can I get them to focus in class when there is so much I cannot control or change?" Ms. Martinez switched to Garza because she heard about the solution focused approach and believed she could learn to be more helpful to her students; the idea of being able to solution build with students gave her a new sense of purpose and hope.

When Ms. Martinez walked into Garza for her interview, she noticed student artwork in the hallways; students wearing punk or eccentric clothes; and teachers smiling, walking the hallways in a relaxed and joyful manner. These were noticeable differences from her previous position at a school with a strict dress code, where teachers oftentimes had stressed looks on their faces, and the hallways were empty. Once she began teaching at

Garza, it was clear how differently teachers approached conversations with students there. Furthermore, teachers, parents, counselors, and administrators were extremely collaborative and communicative with one another. They spoke to and acknowledged one another, generally exhibiting calm and friendly demeanors. They talked about daily goals, small steps forward, and about how each student was able to progress immediately.

These conversations were in stark contrast with the ones in her other positions, where outside of her math team, Ms. Martinez did not get to speak with other professionals at school and where conversations would quickly take on a pessimistic or sarcastic outlook. Though Ms. Martinez faced a lot of challenging student interactions at Garza—even more than she did in her previous high school—she learned how to work with students' individual goals, how to remain calm and hopeful, and how to speak to students in a way that would create positive expectancies for change. Rather than feeling overwhelmed, Ms. Martinez said,

> I now feel focused. I know how to support these students toward graduation. I know how to talk to them and how to help. Before I had this huge circle of concern and almost zero influence. Now my circle of concern and circle of influence are more equal. I can help students set goals, communicate with me respectfully, and succeed!

Introduction

Knowing how to set goals and positive expectancies for success, as well as how to support positive emotions, such as hope, is very important to the change processes of Solution Focused Brief Therapy (SFBT) (Kim & Franklin, 2015; Reiter, 2010). Talking about goals creates an experience in which students are thinking about what they want and what it takes to move forward. Imagining steps forward helps clarify and activate behaviors that can lead to a more positive future. Hope-filled conversations create positive emotions and help change viewpoints about what is possible. Positive emotions have been shown to improve attention, creativity, and problem-solving, making people more open to new experiences and seeing their way through challenges, while negative emotions can restrict problem-solving and promote withdrawal and defensive ways of responding (Fitzpatrick & Stalikas, 2008; Garland et al., 2010). Countless studies indicate that expectancies for success predict academic achievement (Pekrun, 2016). Positive expectations can also facilitate the learning process and can affect how teachers view and impact students (Alderman, 2004). This chapter covers the importance of setting goals and creating positive expectancies for success as well as cultivating positive emotions with at-risk adolescents within solution focused alternative high schools. It further shows how goals, positive expectancies for success, and positive emotions can be strategically created with students at the admissions stage of attending an alternative high school and carried on in daily interactions with students in the classrooms.

Setting Goals

Goals and future-oriented expectations drive conversations between students, parents, and staff within a solution focused alternative high school. Students and families are asked to discuss their hopes for what they would like to see happen at the school, and the purpose of these conversations is to set individual goals and to raise expectations for a positive outcome. Prospective students meet personally by appointment with the registrar, who begins engaging the students and families in the collaborative goal-setting process.

Goal setting in SFBT is not an end point that is set and delivered by school staff but one that reflects specific outcomes that a student wants to see happen. Goals are small, attainable, measureable, and include concrete examples of what students want to happen within their everyday lives at the school. Goals are believed to be the beginning of a change process and not an end to be achieved. When formulated in the beginning, goals are aspirational and may even be discussed as a dream. Over time, the steps toward an aspirational goal have to be carefully thought through and discussed in conversations that hone students toward realistic and immediate action steps. The action steps toward goals need to be specific enough to answer the question "Who does what, when, and how?" Because the steps toward goals mostly involve what happens between people, or what others, including the student, can do, we refer to the action steps as *social action steps*.

The idea of a miracle question, which was introduced in Chapter 1, is one way of discovering goals and provides a method for walking students through the details of how their life can be different if their school problems improved. Teachers and other staff may start a conversation with a miracle question by saying,

> Okay, let's imagine that all the educational problems you have been describing [state in the student's own words what the problems are] disappeared tonight while you were sleeping, but you did not know it because you were sleeping. What would be the first thing you would notice that would be different when you woke up?

It will take some patience to walk students through the conversation, but this type of question will help students envision and describe what they want to be different and how that could happen. For example, one student who had trouble getting to school on time said, "I would be getting out of bed in time to get to school on time." That was what the student needed to do. The teacher proceeded to ask a series of questions that would address how this would happen. For example, who, if anyone, was involved in helping the student get up? What small steps in the miracle are already happening? What else would be different once the miracle happened? Who would notice the change?

While thinking through responses to the miracle question, the student communicated answers that involved social action steps and different responses that could help him reach his goal of getting to school on time. He was also able to describe his past successes of when he had been able to get to school on time. This reinforced skills and competencies that he already had. One teacher at Garza offered this example of how she used her own version of the miracle question to help students in her class: The teacher said,

> I ask Carmen what the ideal situation would be if all obstacles to her progress were to be eliminated. She said that her schedule would look different and she would be wearing eyeglasses to help her see and read better. Shortly after our talk she had already changed her schedule and had a pair of glasses.

The scaling question asks students to anchor their experience on a scale, most usually 0–10 or 1–10. Scaling questions can also be used in goal setting to help students anchor a problem and think about how to move forward toward a goal. For example, the first step to using the scale is to depict a problem or concern that the student has discussed using their own words as close as possible on a scale, with 10 being the problem is solved, for example, and 1 being that it is as bad as it has ever been. Once the student has rated themselves on the scale (e.g., 4), then proceed to ask the student what it would take for them to get to the next number (e.g., 5)? The discussion about what would have to happen to get to the next number provides an opportunity to have a solution-building conversation that visualizes and discusses the steps toward the goal. The miracle question can even be incorporated into the scale by first asking the miracle question and then asking the scaling question as a follow-up question. Once the scale is established, you can say something like "let's just suppose some pieces of the miracle were already happening, how would you get to the next number on the scale?" A teacher from Garza offered this example for how she used the scaling question with two students in her classroom:

> I ask Teresa and Olivia, what steps they have accomplished on the shared goal of improving their focus and being more productive, and they both responded that they have had monumental progress, moving from steps 1 to 10 in just one week. Writing down goals at the beginning of the period and using the scaling visual has helped them visualize how much they are progressing, and from there I have observed that they use other strategies to follow through with their plan for the period.

A goal also has to be specific to the student, needs to self-determined, and is set collaboratively with the school staff. The following example was provided retrospectively by a teacher describing a case at Garza. This example shows a student who during a conversation was asked to set a goal but like many students is used to teachers telling her what to do. In this example, the student is encouraged to participate in setting her own goals, and the teacher uses the solution focused questions, miracle question, exception question, and scaling question in the conversation to facilitate ownership of the goal:

Teacher: "Now that you are a part of Garza, what do you think needs to happen to make sure you graduate?"

Student: "I am not sure. I thought you would tell me."

Teacher: "Well, I have seen your school records, but I think you know your life the best and what you hope will happen here to help you graduate."

Student: "I am not good at math. I failed math. I am worried about how I can get through that class. I always thought I wouldn't be able to graduate because of math."

Teacher: "I see. So, you want to be able to pass math here." [Paraphrase of student goal]

Student: "Yeah, I heard this school gives you extra help." [Elaboration of student goal and what the student wants]

Teacher: "Yes, you will not fail here as long as you attend and work hard. You will start where you are and progress from there. How does that sound?"

Student: "That sounds good."

Teacher: "Tell me, was there sometime in the past that you did better in math, even if it was [just] a little bit?" [Exception Question]

Student: "I hate math. I was never very good."

Teacher: "Think hard. There must have been a time when it went a little better."

Long pause

Student: "Okay, in 9th grade I had a teacher that helped me pass a math class. I thought I was going to get an F. I failed every test. She helped me get a C. All the other kids thought it was easy though, because it was a kind of math class for dumb kids. But, I still thought it was hard."

Teacher: "So, you were able to pass with some extra help?"

Student: "Yeah, I had to have help."

Teacher: "Well, I think it was good you were able to do it, because some students are not able to do it even with help. You must have worked hard along with the teacher to make that happen [compliment]. Sounds like you need some more confidence to believe that you can do math."

Student: "Yes, I think that would help."

Teacher: "So, that is a goal. You have to be able to be more confident in math in order to be able to pass."

Student: "Yes."

Teacher: "So, let's start here by doing some math. On a scale of 1 to 10 how confident are you right now that you can get the help you need here at Garza and pass math? [Using a scale to scale confidence]"

Student: "I don't know. Pause. Maybe a 5."

Teacher: "That is great, you are already halfway there. So, how could you move up a point to 6?"

Student: Blank stare. Pause. "I guess I thought you would tell me."

Teacher: "Well, I can probably offer some ideas once I get to know you better but you know yourself and what could help."

Student: "It helped when the teacher would show me how to do it. I can even get the answer right sometime but I don't know how I did it."

Teacher: "Let me see if I've got this right, you like for the teacher to show you the steps for how to do math and when that happens you will be more confident?"

Student: "Yea, that helps."

As seen from this example, goal setting happens in the process of a conversation between a student and teacher or a student and other staff members. Goals also have to be incorporated into a student's daily educational progress. During a student's time at the solution focused alternative high school Garza, the responsibility of the educational process is shared between teacher and student. Every student starts with an aspirational goal to complete high school and proceeds to individualize what is needed to make that happen. Teachers in a solution focused high school operate on an individualized schedule that is developed between teacher and student. Teachers forego dictating academic goals based on average student needs, instead asking what the student believes is practical based on that individual's perspective of his or her own capabilities. Teachers may provide an average frame of reference but just as a platform for joint decision-making, not a rule. Of course, there are still consequences for not meeting certain goals and a set of expectations for work required along a specified timeline. Such goal setting happens in most schools, but the distinction is in individual goals and the ongoing check-ins and solution-building conversations about meeting the goals. Both teachers and students set goals during solution focused conversations and evaluate these for progress, discussing what is working and what needs to be different. Garza adapted SMART goals, which are behavioral and specific, and include a similar goal-setting approach to SFBT. To set a SMART goal, teachers and students have to set a goal that is *specific, measurable, attainable, realistic,* and *time sensitive.* SMART goals are used across academic subjects to set goals toward completing work and graduating. Both students and teachers fill out these forms during a solution-building conversation. The SMART goal sheet that is used at Garza includes every academic subject and helps students, teachers, and other staff envision what is needed to finish courses and to graduate (preferably) on time. SMART goals are not held over a student's head but are used as a piloting tool to gauge steps toward graduation. Both student and teacher can easily look at the goal sheet and talk about what is going well and other steps that are needed. Figure 4.1 shows an example of a SMART goal sheet.

Teachers at Garza see interactions with students as an essential part of building a relationship and an alliance toward the accomplishment of goals through daily check-ins. The SMART goal form described earlier may be used as a point of reference. Scaling questions are also used by teachers during this daily check-in to track and envision new steps of progress. For example, a teacher may ask a student, "How would you rate your progress toward graduation on a scale of 1 to 10, with 10 being graduating tomorrow?" If a student consistently rates this at 2, it may be an indication to the teacher that the student is not feeling hopeful. For students who make progress more slowly, scaling motivation before scaling behavior is a way

Student Name: Jane Doe
Student ID: 1369465
Six Weeks: (1) 2 3 4 5 6 7

Per.	Class	Teacher	Progress Status Shade in Completion of each Block			Start Date	Optional Comments	Initials
1	English 3A	Rees	A	B	C	July 14		CR
2	Math Models A	Nunnally	A	B	C	July 14		RN
3	Art II	Andrews	A	B	C	July 14	Great job! ☺	DA
4	Physics PAP	Howard	A	B	C	July 14	Needs to ask for help	NH
5	US History A	Valencia	A	B	C	July 14	Slowed down	BV

2016-2017 Six Weeks 1st= 8/22-9/30 2nd= 10/3-11/10 3rd= 11/11-12/20 4th=1/4-2/14 5th=2/15-4/7 6th=4/10-6/1 7th=6/12-7/27

---------- to be completed in Ujamaa ----------

Creating SMART goals: (S-Specific, M-Measurable, A-Attainable, R-Realistic, T-Time Sensitive)

1. What assignments, units, or courses can you finish by October 21st (the Friday we leave for Fall break)?
   - Finish art
   - Get through Block "A" in US History A
   - Talk to Ms. Howard about moving to Physics from Pre-AP Physics
2. What do you plan to accomplish before November 18th (the Friday before Thanksgiving break)?
   - Change schedule
   - Finish English (set goals to stay on track)
   - Math models – starting Block C
3. What do you plan to accomplish before December 9th (final date to turn in work for GPA ranking, senior status upgrade, etc.)?

I must be done with these 1st semester courses by Dec to stay on track. Ms. Valencia and Mr. Rees are really working on goal setting every two weeks. Attendance is sometimes an issue because of life at home, but I work on staying focused on school

Figure 4.1 SMART Goal Check-Ins.

to compliment them on their progress or intentions. As a result, on a scale of 1–10 (with 1 being "I am not sure I am ready to work that hard on it right now" and 10 being "I would do anything to finish history in time to graduate in the spring") a teacher may ask, "Where would you rate yourself today?" By using these scaling questions, teachers can note students' perception of progress and motivation rather than their own conception of progress. When a student does meet a self-set goal, the teacher compliments the student's accomplishments. Box 4.1 further shows how a teacher interacts with a student in a solution-building conversation around goals.

Box 4.1 Teacher's Daily Interaction with a Student

When Sara walked into Mr. William's office she had a scowl on her face. She was dressed in the clothes she had worn the day before, and the skin under her eyes appeared dark. She sat down in an empty chair and placed her head down on the desk. All the other students were at their desks, working independently. Mr. Williams was walking around the classroom stopping to check on each student. When he reached Sara's desk he pulled up a chair and began to talk.

Mr. Williams: "Good morning, Sara."

Sara: "Ugh! I don't want to talk Mr. Williams; I could barely get out of bed this morning."

Mr. Williams: "It's hard to get up in the morning and face the day. I appreciate you being here. I know it's not easy to come to school every day, but you've come to school every day for the past two weeks. It's a big deal and I hope you know that."

Sara: "I feel so sad all the time and I just don't see myself getting better. I'm not making progress with my depression and I'm not making progress here."

Mr. Williams: "Where do you feel yourself making progress?"

Sara: "I think my mom and I are better, she is really supportive of me being here and I only came today because I know that it will make her happy."

Mr. Williams: "Your mom is right, being here is the first step. Your goal last week was to come to school every day and you have done that. You are reaching that goal!"

Sara: "Yeah?"

(Continued)

(Continued)

Mr. Williams: "Yes you have. You just enrolled here at Garza and you have already completed your first goal. What do you see next for yourself?"

Sara: "Starting the assigned book. Just reading it is something I can do."

Mr. Williams: "How much reading do you think you can complete?"

Sara: "Half. I can do half."

Mr. Williams: "Okay, I'll make a note of that. You are moving forward; it may not always feel like it but you are. I see you come to school every day and I am seeing you work. I know you are trying."

Sara: "Okay, thanks. I am really trying."

In this conversation, Mr. Williams used compliments and an exception question to amplify the student's recognition of progress toward her goal. This particular student, Sara had just enrolled at Garza and had a diagnosis of major depressive disorder (MDD). Her symptoms made it difficult for her to succeed in a traditional high school and had strained her relationships with her mother. Sara's enrollment at Garza was a relief not just for her but for her mother as well. Although the goals of (1) attending school and (2) reading the assigned book seem like small goals, they were, for Sara, essential steps toward graduation. In this example, Mr. Williams adopted a core relationship value of SFBT: to meet the students where they are.

Positive Expectancies and Positive Emotions for Success

At a solution focused alternative high school, the integration of positive expectancies and positive emotions for success into a student's experience begins even before the first day. Upon admittance to the school, students are told they will become part of a limited and, in a way, elite community. These types of communications begin to shape the viewpoints and positive emotions of students. From the very beginning and through purposefully crafted conversations, the administrators, teachers, counselors, and other staff raise expectations toward a student's educational success through the communication of hope and a sense of purpose and destiny in the student's decision to come to the school.

One way this can be done is through compliments about the student's choice to come to the school and acting impressed about being accepted. Staff might say, "You got in here! Wow! That is not so easy to do." As was discussed in Chapter 1, compliments in SFBT are more than praise or pointing out positive attributes. In general, compliments are used strategically to help students recognize their own competencies and to change the way they view themselves. Compliments can also be used to highlight motivation and past or present effort toward goals to complete a students' education as well as point out how characteristics such as persistence and coping have helped a student. For example, staff can offer compliments for the effort a student made to follow through with a referral from a previous high school and come for an interview. Indirect compliments can also be made; for example, "Sometimes there is a waiting list so, good job getting an interview." Staff may also ask students "What made you decide to come?" or "What made you decide you would be a good fit here?" These kinds of conversations where staff ask questions that solicit students to discuss their own accomplishments can help students to take pride in their own accomplishments and raise their own hopeful expectations for success. This is demonstrated in the following example that was described retrospectively by a counselor at Garza.

Counselor: "So, tell me: What are you good at?"
Student: "Art. I really like to draw and paint, but I can do lots of different kinds of art."
Counselor: "So, what is your best art?"
Student: "Drawing."
Counselor: "What do you like to draw?"
Student: "It is hard to describe. Abstract images and ideas. I like lots of colors and street art. I like to draw tattoos too."
Counselor: "Wow! So, you are good at drawing ideas and body art images?"
Student: "I think so. I want to be. I won a few contests."
Counselor: "You won some contests. I did not know that. Well, sounds like you are good at art! What is the best thing that ever happened that made you believe in yourself as an artist?"
Student: "I won a statewide contest last year and got honorable mention in a regional one."
Counselor: "So, that really spoke to you that you are good at art."
Student: (Smiles and nods.) "Yeah, I love to do art."
Counselor: "So, who else believes you are good at art?"

Counselor: "My former art teacher told me I was good."

Counselor: "Of course! She recognizes the talents in her students. Who else?"

Student: "All of my teachers and friends I have drawn tattoos for."

Counselor: "Of course. This gives you a lot of confidence then. What else are you good at besides art?"

Counselor: "That is it, mostly art. I just want to do art. I want to go to the Art Institute in Chicago."

Counselor: "That's where you want to go to college?"

Student: "Yes, it is just a great place to be."

Counselor: "Wow! That is a big goal. Sounds like you already know what you want to do and what you are good at."

Student: "Yes."

Counselor: "So, what is it about this school that made you believe it was a good fit for you?"

Student: "I liked all the art that was around the school. I like the mural. Just the feel of the place. How you can work at your own pace and there is less stress. I thought I could graduate from here."

Counselor: "So, you like the art feel of the school, the self-paced curriculum, and believe you can graduate from here. Great! How confident are you that you can graduate from here?"

Student: "Pretty confident. I like it because I can work at my own pace."

Counselor: "I see you need 10 academic credits. On a scale of 1–10, how confident are you that you can finish those credits as well as doing art?"

Student: "Hm. I don't know. Maybe 7."

Counselor: "That is pretty high. How did you get to be so confident?"

Student: "I just feel that way because I got accepted here and because of the way the school is. I think I can do the credits. Anyway, I want to graduate so I can go to Chicago."

Counselor: "Well, you certainly have a good reason to finish your credits. I am glad you are so confident this school is a good fit for you and you can finish high school here."

In this example, the counselor used a focus on the student's perceived strengths, indirect compliments, and a scaling question from SFBT to help the student provide self-compliments. This solution-building conversation acknowledges the competencies of the student and the commitment toward finishing high school.

Creating a Success Story

It is important for staff to help students create a success story that can be shared with others in the alternative high school. Positive stories about a student that are told within a school community can help both students and staff stay focused on goals and positive expectancies for success. This type of solution-building conversation requires purposefully listening to the stories of students to help craft hopeful and successful stories about their futures. By listening carefully for student strengths and positive changes, teachers, counselors, social workers, and other school staff will be able to co-construct hopeful stories with students that are filled with strengths and positive expectancies for graduating. The following example was told retrospectively by a school social worker who worked with a Garza student and shows this kind of listening and solution-building conversation that can lead to a success story being built around a student.

Social Worker: "So, what was your best hope that brought you here?"

Student: "I dropped out when I got pregnant and my grandma was helping me. I wanted to go all the way through high school. I told my grandma I would finish."

Social Worker: "So, you want to finish school and coming here makes that possible. I bet your grandma is proud of you."

Student: "Yeah, she told me she was really proud I got in here."

Social Worker: "I bet you may be a little proud of yourself too because it takes a lot of effort to get in here."

Student: (Smiles.) "I guess so. I am really glad I am here."

Social Worker: "So, I want to know a little more about your story. Tell me how you managed to get in here?"

Student: "Well, one of my counselors had told me about the school before I had my baby. So, I kept putting it off because I was pretty sick during parts of my pregnancy and I was trying to deal with a lot of things. I was fighting with the baby's daddy and then he got thrown in jail. I didn't know what to do. I was homeless for a little while but my grandma took me in. After the baby came I thought about calling to see if I could get in."

Social Worker: "You have been through a lot. Yet you still wanted to finish high school. You are really an amazing young mother."

Student: (Smiles.) "I don't know. Yeah, I want a better life for me and my baby. I wanted to finish school. I also talked it over with my friend who graduated from here who told me it was a great place. That made me want to come."

Social Worker: "So, you wanted to finish high school here and know this is the right place for you. You agree with your friend. Sounds like you have a lot of motivation. You want to be here."

Student: "Yeah, the school has child care and that is one reason too. My grandma works and can't always help me take care of the baby. I like the idea of coming here and bringing my baby. I will have to bring my baby on the public bus because I don't have a way to get here, but I think it is worth it."

Social Worker: "What? You are bringing your baby on the bus to attend? You really *do* want to come here and finish school! I am really impressed with your decisions. You are already making a better life for you and your baby."

In this case, the student's story was co-constructed and shaped in a conversation with the school social worker. Her motivation and desire to be in the school and her willingness to work hard to bring her baby on the bus were highlighted. Although it was not an easy journey, this particular student eventually graduated from Garza. She continued to bring her baby on a bus so she could attend the school, and her efforts and hard work were frequently complimented. The idea of bringing the baby on the public bus was used as a metaphor for the student's efforts to be a good student and mother, and became a part of her success story within the school. All the teachers and other staff at Garza knew the story and repeated it often to one another and in the presence of the student. This "baby on the bus" story was also used to increase hope and to support the student, even at times when she was struggling and taking some steps backwards. The staff communicated the story and told her how they were so impressed with her. She had what it took to finish high school because she had made progress, even though it was not easy. When the student graduated from Garza, the principal once again told the story of how she had finished her diploma despite the fact that she had to bring the baby on the bus.

Positive Perceptions of Education within the Alternative School

Nothing shapes positive perceptions more than positive experiences. From the first day at a solution focused alternative high school, staff communicate the importance of being accepted into the school as being analogous to winning a prestigious award, even when most students have never won anything prior to that point. As one student, Jamal, noted,

> I had never been part of anything before. I have been in the foster care system for so long and moved from school to school. I was in no clubs and a part of nothing. To be accepted into the solution focused high school was huge for me. It felt like I was welcomed.

Another student, Ramon, said,

> I was told all of my life that I was going to turn up like my dad. A drunk with no education. My thoughts and my doings were always negative until I came to Garza. Being with negative people helps you become negative and being with positive people helps you become positive. Garza was always and will be positive and for that it has made me more positive in my behavior and my being.

During a research interview, another student, Skye, had this to say about her experiences in the school:

> It's the environment. It changes everybody here. I'm really proud of this school. I'm really glad I go here. Just being part of the whole school. The whole school has made the difference in my desire to go to college. I have made straight As here and the career center has helped a lot.

Some educators may minimize entrance to an alternative school or may even consider high school graduation from an alternative high school to be a bare minimum expectation for graduation. These kinds of beliefs will not be useful to at-risk students like the ones that are quoted earlier. In contrast, the staff in a solution focused alternative high school communicate pride in the school and confidence in its curriculum. They want their students to feel the pride and do the same. It is important to never minimize effort toward the goal of graduation. One teacher at Garza said,

> I am a teacher here but I am also a parent. At home my kids pass classes and will graduate high school with little trouble. But my kids are privileged, they don't have a learning disability, they have affluent parents and are supported by their community. A lot of my students come from very little. When you come from nothing, getting yourself through the eighth grade and into high school may be a big deal. Some of my students are the first people in their family to make it past the eighth grade. Even though it's not my reality, that work and effort is something I have to acknowledge and validate.

While attending a solution focused alternative high school, students never move backwards and are never asked to repeat classes due to learning gaps. In recognition of the fact that they have advanced this far, they continue to move forward, passing classes and earning current credits. This type of approach to student progress helps keep positive expectancies for success and hope alive. The staff recognize that many students pursue an alternative setting due to exceptionally challenging personal circumstances or the inability of their previous schools to support their unique learning needs. Alternative school students who have fallen through gaps along the way may have undiagnosed learning challenges and in the past scraped by only to reach a crisis point. They come to school lacking skills and confidence in their academic abilities. This does not mean, however, that they are incapable of building educational solutions from where they are at present. But it does mean that allowing them to focus on past failures can create anxiety and fear, if not outright defensiveness and hostility. Such negative emotions will detract from solution-building. This is why students are guided forward from where they are currently, and their academic challenges and past educational problems are de-emphasized.

In the solution focused alternative school, you begin where the student is and move forward in a way that offers hope, decreasing stress. One Garza student, Roxanne explained in a research interview how this type of approach helped her continue to persist toward graduating. Roxanne said,

> The school has eased a lot of my stress from life, especially during my depression. People here really do care. I don't have any stress about school anymore. When I was depressed I didn't want to come to school but I did. The teachers really helped me out a lot... That was a big reason why I didn't drop out... I'm so close to graduating. My teacher helped me out and helped me realize I didn't need to drop out just because I'm sad.

We have found that meeting each student where they are and moving forward from that starting point also reduces the anxiety and anger from concerned parents, who are used to schools emailing, calling, and summoning their presence to deliver bad news about their students' problem behaviors and academic failures. Instead, in the solution focused school, the staff provide strengths-based reports to parents. Of course, sometimes, it is necessary and important to bring up problems. Nonetheless, during those times staff still maintain a friendly and positive outlook, always beginning communications with compliments about the student.

Staff also realize that some parents are overwhelmed with their own problems and pressuring them about their child will not lead to a solution. Instead, it is the intention of the leadership and staff to change the conversation at the dinner table, which will invariably lessen the arguments and negative emotions around school. The following Garza student described in a research interview how her attendance at the school affected her relationship with her mother.

Interviewer: "Is there anything about coming to Garza that helped change your relationship with your mother?"

Student: "She's not as 'at me' because other teachers [at the student's old school] used to gripe about everything. And they [Garza teachers] are more open. I guess in that way it's improved because she's always been worried about school. Coming here eased it up a bit."

Interviewer: "On a scale of 1 to 10, how well did you get along with your parents before coming to Garza?"

Student: "Six."

Interviewer: "On a scale of 1 to 10, how well do you get along now?"

Student: "Nine or 10."

Interviewer: "How is it that your relationship has improved?"

Student: "Everything is more open now. I'm not trying to hide report cards or anything. She [the student's mother] notices the progress I'm making."

Interviewer: "Why do you think you can talk to her about these things now as opposed to before?"

Student: "Before, I was always in trouble. Here, they don't accept a low grade. You just keep trying and improve your grade. At regular school you always get a low grade no matter what, because you have eight classes going on. She would always gripe about grades. Here they don't let you fail."

An Example of a Solution Focused Conversation

One day, Selena came into class angry and hostile. Her whole body was tense, and she had a frown. After seeing Selena walk in Mr. Rodriguez said, "Selena login to the computer, you will see your next assignment waiting for you. You're almost half way down with this credit!"

Selena turned fiercely at Mr. Rodriguez, "I am not in the mood right now so please shut up."

Mr. Rodriguez took a deep breath and walked away from Selena. He did not know what upset her so much, but it was clear that engaging with her would only amplify her frustration.

Ten minutes later, Mr. Rodriguez noticed that Selena's mood had changed, she was now crying. He walked over to her and asked if she would like to step outside for a moment. Selena nodded. After walking outside the classroom Mr. Rodriguez said, "I noticed that you were upset when you walked into class and that you are unhappy now. What are you feeling right now?"

Selena looked up at Mr. Rodriguez and said bitterly, "I have not finished my English credit! I am so angry at this school right now. I just want to be done!"

"I can see you are anxious to be finished with school and I'm hearing that you are feeling behind and you are not where you want to be" replied Mr. Rodriguez. Selena remained silent and nodded. "When have you felt good about your work here?" asked Mr. Rodriguez.

"When I finish something! But it's just too hard to get to the end of assignments every week so I feel like I keep failing," said Selena.

> Ah, I am hearing that finishing an assignment every week is too large of a goal. These assignments are extensive Selena; I wouldn't expect you to finish them all in a week's time. How about we discuss your goals in this class?

After setting smaller and more reasonable goals for herself, Selena began to feel better about her progress. When she set the goal of finishing an assignment a week, Mr. Rodriguez felt that the goal was not practical. However, Selena was determined to make that her standard. Rather than argue with her about her defined goals, he allowed Selena to make the decision and found opportunities to reinforce her setting more realistic standards for herself.

Key Points to Keep in Mind

- Goals, positive expectancies for success, and the cultivation of positive emotions, such as hope, are integral to the success of a solution focused alternative high school program.
- A goal is not an end point but the beginning of a change process.
- Meeting students and their families where they are at present means setting goals that are achievable. For example, if a student has difficulty attending class, the first goal should not be "pass a math test." Rather, set a smaller goal that is on the path to passing a math test.
- A miracle question is a solution focused question that can be used to help a student discover a goal.
- Students and teachers work together on daily educational goals, which are discussed in the classroom.
- Positive expectancies for graduating begin during admissions and continue as each staff member puts forth an explicit effort to build solutions with students and make meaningful and personal contact with students the first priority.
- Compliments can be strategically used to support positive expectancies for success and to cultivate positive emotions and competencies in students.
- It is important for students and parents to have a positive perception of education within a solution focused alternative school.
- Effort toward graduating from an alternative school should always be viewed positively and outwardly acknowledged.
- Positive experiences in an alternative school can lessen stress for students and parents, resulting in positive emotions and better relationships.

Summary

Establishing goals and positive expectancies for success, as well as cultivating positive emotions are important to the change processes in SFBT. This chapter discusses the importance of setting goals and positive expectancies for success and how to support positive emotions, such as hope. It gives examples of how to set goals in solution focused conversations, including how to discuss daily goals in the classroom. A SMART goal sheet that is used in a solution focused high school has been provided. Explicit examples of how to increase positive expectancies and emotions toward success are also provided, along with how positive emotions can facilitate the learning process and affect how teachers, students, and parents interact. Creating a success story with a student that can be shared within the school community is one technique that can be used for creating hope and positive expectancies for graduation. Specific examples of solution focused conversations between teachers and students, counselors and students, and social workers and students are further offered to illustrate the concepts discussed in the chapter.

Note

1 Cases presented in this chapter are taken from research interviews of students that attend an alternative high school and staff experiences working with these students. Names and some information have been changed to protect the confidentiality of the students involved. Some of these interviews were made possible by the generous support of the Hogg Foundation for Mental Health at The University of Texas at Austin.

References

Alderman, M. K. (2004). *Motivation for achievement: Possibilities for teaching and learning*. Mahwah, NJ: Lawrence Erlbaum.

Fitzpatrick, M. R., & Stalikas, A. (2008). Positive emotions as generators of therapeutic change. *Journal of Psychotherapy Integration, 18*, 137–154. doi:10.1037/1053-0479.18.2.137

Garland, E. L., Fredrickson, B., Kring, A. M., Johnson, D. P., Meyer P. S., & Penn, D. L. (2010). Upward spirals of positive emotions counter downward spirals of negativity: Insights from the broaden-and-build theory and affective neuroscience on the treatment of emotion dysfunctions and deficits in psychopathology. *Clinical Psychology Review, 30*, 849–864. doi:10.1016/j.cpr.2010.03.002

Kim, J. S., & Franklin, C., (2015). The use of positive emotion in solution-focused brief therapy. *Best Practices in Mental Health, 11*(1), 25–41. doi: 10.3534839

Pekrun, R. (2016). Academic emotions. In K. R. Wentzel & D. B. Miele (Eds.), *Handbook of motivation at school, second edition* (pp. 120–144). New York, NY: Routledge.

Reiter, M. D. (2010). Hope and expectancy in solution-focused brief therapy. *Journal of Family Psychotherapy, 21*(2), 132–148. doi:10.1080/08975353.2010.483653

5

How to Create a Solution Focused Student Support Team

A Story to Get Started

Despite her pregnancy, Shana[1] had been trying for some time to focus on doing what normal 16-year-old girls do. Rather than emphasizing her past, she saw moving to a solution focused high school as an opportunity for her to attend a school that focused on her ability to achieve the future she wanted. However, transferring to a new school was not the magical solution to all of life's problems. Shana still had doctor's appointments to go to, physical discomforts to deal with, and planning to do for the hugely complex years to come.

Shana transferred to Gonzalo Garza Independence High School and was just the type of student the school was designed for. Despite her obstacles, she was passionate about learning and motivated to graduate. Shana's teachers, counselor, school nurse, social worker, and administrators were well aware of her pregnancy and adjusted her academics accordingly. This did not mean simply providing extra restroom breaks or making sure she could complete her coursework before her due date. This also meant allowing Shana to set self-paced goals regarding her coursework and school attendance.

To help Garza's staff assist Shana, designated staff members who served on a collaborative student support team (SST) had an opportunity to check in with one another and with Shana to review her changing needs and ensure that her goals were achievable. During these meetings, the staff focused on Shana's existing solutions rather than problems. For example, if Shana found it difficult to complete homework on the day of a medical appointment, teachers focused on Shana's previous attendance at after-school homework help groups and her past motivation rather than her pregnancy.

Initially, Shana had worried about feeling shamed by others for being young and pregnant, and transferring to an alternative school to try and finish her education; however, she quickly realized that the school's staff were aligned with her goals and needs. Although her academic pace fluctuated throughout the semester as she made more doctors' appointments, the SST was able to work with Shana to keep her goals current and to help her find her own solutions to challenges. Shanna felt supported and was focused on her present goal of graduating.

Introduction

In order to create a solution focused approach that is effective in alternative schools, it is necessary to create transdisciplinary teams in which all staff members change the way they think about collaboration. Mutual respect and trust between different disciplines is essential, and staff members are required to develop a sense of shared knowledge and responsibility for the team's work (Streeter & Franklin, 2002). The solution focused team is a collaborative one, and the principles for how to build relationships that are practiced within Solution Focused Brief Therapy (SFBT) still apply. However, the focus has changed from individual and family work to teamwork among professionals. The solution-building approach can also facilitate the success of transdisciplinary teams within alternative schools because the principles of solution focused communication (e.g., solution-talk) are practiced between the different professionals. In addition, the emphasis on intentional and purposeful listening and focus on strengths facilitate collaboration with students, parents, and teachers, all of whom work together on practical solutions to problems.

Other solution focused principles also serve as a basis for teamwork. For example, the systems perspective that different approaches may result in solutions and the importance of showing respect for the unique ideas, beliefs, and styles of others involved with the student are both integral to successful teamwork (Murphy & Duncan, 2007). Mutual respect and open-mindedness between different professionals are both pieces of the collaborative mind-set involved in a solution focused team. While these principles from SFBT have a strong philosophical and values base, it is important that respectful and strengths-oriented beliefs be translated into action.

This chapter illustrates how to create solutions using a collaborative SST within an alternative high school. Specifically, this chapter shows how different disciplines can participate together in a weekly, solution-building conversation and meeting aimed at developing individual solutions for students who are referred for a discussion. Nuts and bolts information about how to convene the participants and operate the meeting is also provided, along with techniques and principles for how to develop a transdisciplinary team using SFBT.

Collaborative Teamwork on a Solution Focused Campus

Implementation of a collaborative SST within a solution focused alternative school brings together individuals dedicated to providing individualized consideration of each student's unique challenges and needs. Solution-building facilitates a collaborative approach in four important ways. First, the underlying principles of solution-building, such as viewing others as experts, focusing on strengths, and collaborating to create solutions, foster an openness to incorporating the ideas of others (Franklin, Moore & Hopson, 2008). Second, the fact that teachers and other staff members are all trained in solution-building creates an environment in which all staff members understand the solution focused change principles, making it easier for instructional staff to work together with noninstructional support staff. Third, the focus on solution-building gives teachers the skills and confidence needed to collaborate with mental health professionals, and the team approach helps mental health professionals better understand the necessity of classroom instruction, developing their respect for the knowledge and expertise of teachers. Shared knowledge and goals provide the basis for the mutual respect needed for staff to work together to develop solutions. Finally, mutual training and cooperation within the team creates a common foundation of knowledge and a similar language that improves shared communications and solution-building among the staff. The transdisciplinary teamwork between everyone creates a cooperative relational atmosphere that will become contagious. This atmosphere transfers to the climate of the school and allows staff to work successfully with students.

This is not to say that it is easy to build a transdisciplinary team within an alternative school; in fact, it can be very challenging. But the hard work of building a transdisciplinary team is in itself part of what makes the school successful as professionals learn to agree and work together with each other, adolescents, and parents to forge solutions (Franklin & Guz, 2017).

One practical method for the development of a team in an alternative school is using the transdisciplinary approach to create an SST that uses SFBT to address student issues. The SST overlaps and supports the work of noninstructional staff members, such as counselors, social workers, and teachers who may participate on the SST. Although the team is drawn from separate disciplines, the best productivity occurs when all team members, regardless of discipline or roles, actively participate and focus on a future solution rather than complaints or frustrations about a student. The SST recognizes that the solution may already exist within the resources and strengths of the student, allowing the team to build a solution that matches the student. The team also identifies resources, whether they are a student's family members or outside community agencies that the student visits. It is important for the team to implement the internal and surrounding resources as a critical part of building and maintaining a solution. When discussing difficult student cases, it is easy to become punitive or judgmental; however, these pitfalls are unproductive for the team and for the student.

In pre-planned, weekly scheduled meetings, the SST gathers to discuss each student individually because solutions are viewed as being unique to the individual, and as a result, each approach will be different. One student may benefit from social work and community services as a solution, while another student may utilize student-teacher conferences or peer mentoring. Throughout the SST meeting, the team members remain optimistic, emotions expressed toward each student are hopeful and positive, and the focus of conversation is placed on the present and future. This requires discipline from each team member and a willingness to practice a solution focused mind-set. Different team members advocate for the student, provide compliments to one another, and acknowledge the student's abilities. After discussing a student, the team does not conclude without first identifying at least one action step, which may be as small as continuing to monitor the student's progress or as large as restructuring the student's class schedule. The team takes an immediate action step, knowing that if one solution does not work, they will resolve to find another one that will. Individual students are promptly contacted and brought into the solution focused conversation, where the solutions suggested by the SST may be negotiated further and revisited at the next or subsequent meetings. The implementation of the SST is described and illustrated in more detail in the following.

Implementation of a Collaborative SST

This transdisciplinary team contains representatives from every area, including counselors and social workers, teachers, administrators, and even representatives from the school district or community agencies who may bring outside resources to the table. See Box 5.1 for examples of the types of team members who can serve on the SST within a solution focused alternative school.

Box 5.1 Examples of SST Team Members

Who is on the Student Support Services Team at Garza?

- Principal
- Assistant Principal
- 504 Coordinator
- Outreach Specialist
- School Social Worker
- Special Education Teacher
- Dropout Prevention Specialist
- Teacher Representative
- Technology Specialist
- Communities In Schools Representative
- Members present on occasion or as needed:
- Nurse
- District School Psychologist

Transdisciplinary team members come together to review, reflect on, discuss, and develop solutions for any student issues that might arise. The SST deals with any irregularities in student performance, behavior, or attendance. While staff members undergo specialized training to identify behavioral risk factors correlated with issues such as depression and suicidal ideation, the staff in a solution focused alternative school take steps to identify smaller concerns that may signal that something is not right. Examples of these signals are changes in a student's attentiveness, a sharp decline in a student's performance, or a sudden personality or mood change, all of which may be observed in the classroom.

One Garza student serves as an example of how teachers were able to be responsive to a student's signs of a depressive episode and, as a result, increase their support. The student said,

> When I came to Garza I liked the small class sizes. I just like the whole idea of the school, that the kids and teachers are here because they want to be. And people acknowledge that sometimes we have bad days and we were struggling with stuff outside of school. At my previous school people don't take that into consideration. It's stress free because teachers are paying attention to me and noticing when I need more support. I have no stress because of school anymore.

In the case of this particular student, staff noticed her crying often in class, coming to school late or being absent, saying she felt worthless, and not being able to socialize with her peers. These behaviors were not typical for the student, and when the student was reviewed at the SST, the counselor disclosed that the student's parents had informed her earlier in the week about the student's diagnosis of major depressive disorder (MDD). The diagnosis was given to her by a psychiatrist at a community mental health agency a year earlier. The counselor on the team then raised the point that major depressive disorder includes episodes during which individuals experience symptoms more severely. As a result, the team decided that rather than punishing the student for her perceived misconduct and for missing assignments and school, they would instead increase support for the student by intensifying their positive interactions with her. The team also made sure that the student set up an appointment with a social worker in the school. The change in support was small, but the student felt the difference; in a subsequent interview, she said,

> Garza has eased a lot of my stress from life, especially during my depression. People here really do care. I don't have any stress about school anymore. When I was depressed I didn't want to come to school but I did. The teachers really helped me out a lot. If I needed to go home to be by myself I could. One of my teachers would say, 'Do what you

> can and I'll let you leave early.' That was a big reason why I didn't drop out... I'm so close to graduating. My teacher helped me out and helped me realize I didn't need to drop out just because I'm sad. Garza definitely makes dealing with crises easier.

Teachers, counselors, social workers, and other school staff are all involved in identifying and addressing items of concern among individual students. When staff members witness signals that demonstrate stress or abrupt changes in a student's behavior, they treat it like a wake-up call. This results in engaging the student. It may also result in a possible referral to the SST, and anyone can submit a referral at any time. Some schools are fortunate enough to have school-based services or crisis teams that are equipped to intervene with a student crisis or a serious problem that may arise. But instead of relying on specialized mental health teams, all the teachers within a solution focused alternative school are prepared to respond to the immediate emotional needs of students. When problems persist, teachers and other staff make referrals to the SST. When referrals are received, the job of the SST is to remain solution focused by: (1) remaining present and future focused, (2) identifying existing solutions or what has worked well in past solutions, and (3) keeping a social action and relational focus.

Remaining Present Focused and Identifying Existing Solutions

Solutions are always defined and provided with a common goal of understanding what is currently happening with a student and with the hope of engaging that student in a solution that will work in the current circumstances. If that understanding leads to being able to help and come up with a solution or the start of a solution, then the team is functioning as intended. The SST not only works to address existing situations but also to prevent the development of serious problems. Students who are not in crisis or do not demand immediate attention often do not receive it, but the team knows that many students may suffer in silence and that small steps backward with an adolescent can quickly escalate to an emergency situation. What is important is to be attuned to behavior in the present. As a result, the alternative school staff carefully observe the reactions of each student and constantly checks in with students about their lives. They then make referrals to the SST to correct small steps backward that may lead to problems in a student's school performance down the road.

Once the SST receives a referral, it takes steps to remain present-focused and to identify existing solutions that may work in the future. One example of how the team is prompted to stay solution focused is with the *statement of purpose* read at the beginning of each meeting. When the statement of purpose is read aloud it becomes a time for the team to explicitly state why they are there. It is not enough to simply know that everyone present wants to help the student in question. Stating the reason out loud solidifies the intention behind the work the team intends to complete together. That statement of purpose can be as simple as "Joining together to find positive solutions that meet the needs of these students." Ultimately, the statement must be oriented around finding solutions and remaining focused in the present and the future. This purpose will frame the statements, actions, and motivations of the team throughout the meeting and when designing the social plan of action. This step serves both to initiate constructive solution-building activities and to refocus the group throughout the process. The team members keep each other on task toward what has successfully worked for this student and what is being proposed to work in the future. It can be easy for the meeting to drift off track and look more like a forum for voicing complaints. When this happens, it is more important than ever for everyone to join in repeating the team purpose and remembering that they have a real responsibility to co-create a solution for the student, instead of spending their time complaining or analyzing problems. This is not to say that problems are not discussed but rather that the discussion of problems should quickly pivot to how to build a solution, with the job of each team member being to add to the solution-building conversation.

Social Action Plan

By the end of the meeting, the team has negotiated a workable solution that is action oriented. Team members identify who will take responsibility for an action plan that is specific and goal oriented. The plan has a social action and relational focus, resulting in specific outcomes, such as who will do what, when, and how. There is also a plan to address follow-up and accountability for the action plan. The action plan lets staff involved with the student know that the school is working with the student to move forward. This accountability is a solution focused principle, as the action plan is reasonable and practical. An action plan should not be filled with expectations that are unreasonable or that do not address the current problem. For example, if the student is not attending classes then it would be unreasonable for the solutions in the action plan to address the student's graduation date. Instead, the action plan should work to improve the student's attendance.

In the following example, the action plan focuses on the student's current challenges. In this case, the student is unable to attend classes due to a complex work and family schedule. The SST noted that when the student became pregnant, she took a job and has had difficulty coming to class ever since. Therefore, the suggested solution is to refer her to the school counselor to see if readjusting her class schedule is possible (Table 5.1).

TABLE 5.1 Example of Student Action Plan

Action Plan			
Student School ID	*Student Grade Level*	*Referring Source*	*Date*
Referral Reason 1 Example: Poor attendance	Points Discussed Example: The student has not attended school consistently. It is noted that the student stopped coming to class after she became pregnant and got a job. Possible solution: Readjusting the student's class schedule to make the balance of family, work, and school more practical and manageable.	Referrals Made Example: Referral made to the school counselor to discuss readjusting the student's class schedule to better fit her work schedule.	Follow-Up (Yes or No) Example: Yes, discuss student at next week's SST meeting. Report whether or not an adjustment in student's schedule has been helpful.
Referral Reason 2			
Referral Reason 3			

The Team Meeting

The SST meets once a week after the regular school day. The team is normally in session for three to five hours. To many educators in alternative schools who already feel overburdened with student issues and strapped for time, this may seem like a large commitment. But when one considers the instructional time teachers lose in the classroom to address these same concerns, the result may seem well worth the investment. By addressing the needs of students in a formal team meeting, teachers spend less time correcting behavior in the classroom, while administrators spend less time in disciplinary roles. Within the meeting itself, setting appropriate and clear expectations provides a standard of efficiency that will allow even a long meeting to be a productive one.

The SST usually begins by establishing official duties, such as assigning a facilitator who guides the conversation. The facilitator ensures that the team remains solution focused and works toward finding productive solutions for students, rather than talking off course or becoming negative about a student. In the following dialogue, the facilitator at Garza detailed the role of the facilitator during the SST meeting:

Teacher: "I just don't know, I mean this student dropped out and left the school and is now enrolled. What are we going to do with her in the classroom?"

Counselor: "I totally get your concern; I have reached out to her twice to meet with me so we can create a class schedule for her but she just isn't getting back to me."

Mental Health Specialist: "I don't think I ever saw this student for services, why hasn't anyone referred her to us?"

Teacher: "I know we have been here for close to 40 minutes and that this is our last student case. I know it is a difficult case however, this conversation has gotten a little off track. How did you [Counselor] reach out her to schedule a meeting?"

Counselor: "I spoke to her when I saw her in the hall. She seemed to forget that she had a meeting."

Teacher: "I am wondering if this student needs an agenda or calendar to help her remember dates. Could we get her one?

Also maybe we could try sending her a note the class period before the meeting to reminder her?"

Counselor: "Okay sure. I will send her a note and have an agenda ready to give her when I see her."

At a meeting where teamwork, collaboration, and openness drive the conversation, it is extremely important that expectations do not extend to specific and non-mission-related positions. A job is an assignment that comes with a description, obligation, and limits. True collaboration may best be nurtured in an environment of equal responsibility and participation unhindered by the boundaries of a job title. However, some team members will have roles that come with their regular positions. It is important to distinguish between an individual's duty within the team and the role outside of the team. Roles largely refer to responsibilities that occur before the meeting so that the meeting runs smoothly and proceeds in a way that ensures the group can address all necessary students and their concerns. For example, the role of the Technology Specialist is to set up the computer and screen prior to the meeting so that the meeting can start on time. Within each meeting, these responsibilities fulfill certain group needs before the conversation itself can begin. From this preliminary work, the facts and concerns about the student are brought to the table, and participants are able to apply their own unique perspectives and input to help identify solutions. Table 5.2 illustrates the roles of the SST and a typical meeting agenda.

TABLE 5.2 Roles of SST Members and Typical Meeting Agenda

Team Member	*Responsibilities*	*Purpose*
Counselors	Review and organize student referrals prior to the meeting Identify key facts to present to the team Gather necessary information to supplement information in the referrals	Allows the work to progress efficiently The team can approach each case feeling informed and prepared to suggest solutions appropriate to the student and his or her situation

(*Continued*)

TABLE 5.2 Roles of SST Members and Typical Meeting Agenda (Continued)

Team Member	*Responsibilities*	*Purpose*
Outreach Specialists and Social Workers	Compile and print attendance data (one copy for every team member) for the two weeks prior to the meeting Identify any irregularities that suggest need for review	Changes in attendance often provide the earliest warning signs of problems
Nurse	Review medical needs of students as needed Answer questions about needs and services for students with medical concerns	Provides specific supplemental knowledge when necessary to facilitate the understanding of a wider range of student needs and suggest medically informed solutions
Technology Specialist	Provide a computer and projector for all team members to view photos of each student as the team reviews his or her data	Allows team members who may be unfamiliar with the student to become part of the network of individuals watching that student for risk factors and supporting progress Humanizes the student to avoid seeing him or her as just a case or just a number

A Typical Meeting Agenda:

1 Review the purpose of the meeting to orient everyone to the appropriate mind-set.
2 Review the confidentiality agreement, reminding staff members that everything said in the meeting must remain in the meeting.
3 Everyone receives a copy of the attendance for the last two weeks.
4 Counselors briefly review the list of students to be addressed during the meeting and ask for any other additions.
5 Counselors goes through the list one student at a time, sharing the referral form and necessary background information and asking for discussion of possible solutions.* As each student is introduced, the Technology Specialist projects a picture of that student so that every team member can see the person being discussed. The Outreach Specialist goes over the attendance list to identify potential concerns.
6 The team's decisions are recorded on the forms to be documented and returned to the referring staff member.

*Meetings usually progress in alphabetical order, but team members may be getting tired and more prone to negative input as the meeting progresses, which can result in students at the beginning and end of the alphabet receiving different considerations. Consider taking steps, such as changing up the order between meetings and starting at the end of the alphabet to maintain balance.

Selecting Members of the Solution Focused SST

Not every staff member is willing and able to be a part of this kind of team. Certainly, some of the team members, such as counselors, social workers, and the outreach specialist, are necessary to facilitate the process and work primarily on addressing student needs that interfere with academic performance. However, even though the science teacher may have training in solution focused approaches, this individual will still need to bring the right attitude to every meeting in order to be a productive member of the team. Assembling the appropriate team requires a straightforward conversation and a wholehearted agreement that the staff member is willing and able to enter each meeting and contribute productively.

This includes first acknowledging the agreement to confidentiality. When developing a full view of the life and needs of a student, the team may bring up extremely personal information, much of which the student would never want to become public. All team members commit to keeping everything said in meetings within the confines of that meeting. Staff members may acknowledge that they are just not able to maintain that level of secrecy and as a result may not be the best fit for a team. No subject is off the table for discussion because there is always a chance that an uncomfortable subject could help inform an effective solution. However, much of what the group discusses is not appropriate, and may be damaging, if put on the record; therefore, detailed notes of the meeting are not taken and the meeting is considered confidential. The team should keep in mind that a lot of what they do involves investigation and not the provision of facts. The team should always be thoughtful when considering what information from the meeting should and should not be written down. It is important for the team to consider who the audience of the document is, who will have access to such a document in the future, and what impact reading this document will have on a student's experience moving forward.

Another factor to consider when approaching a staff member about participating in an SST is what reasons that person might have for joining the team. This can involve clarifying with that person the team's statement of purpose and checking that the person is able to honor it as the central focus at all times. If a person wants to join the team to make the workplace environment better for teachers, the match is most likely not a good one. The focus of the meetings is to understand and assist students, not to improve instruction time or promote other self-interests. As mentioned earlier, the meetings can also become long and draining. A staff member who spends the whole meeting worried about getting home to let the dog out will not be focused on the needs of the student being considered. Likewise, a person who struggles to cope emotionally while listening to the personal stories of students may not be able to remain consistently solution oriented. Before agreeing to be a part of the team, every potential team member should understand how a typical meeting proceeds and the potential to encounter prolonged and emotionally demanding evenings of strategic thinking and solution-building.

Anyone willing to join a team that tackles such tough issues when an adolescent's future is at stake is likely to be a passionate individual. Conscientious team building involves identifying and involving people who are fervent about different things in different ways. Anytime a group of individuals with divergent or starkly different views of the situation enter into a collaborative effort, conflict becomes a likely consequence. One team member may think very differently from another, and that may bring up a lot of irritation for both parties. For example, one team member may be more lenient, while one thinks a consequence is never strong enough. Nonetheless, disagreement can result in meaningful conversations and may ensure the most effective solution for a given situation. Building agreement and a commitment for the best way to help adolescents is essential for solution-building. If people in disagreement are focused on the goal of finding a solution, and if they maintain a student-centered approach at all times, the group can recover from disagreements and keep the work on track. This may take some training and practice, but the team must always be able to return to the idea that there is a bigger purpose than resolving personal frustrations and asserting personal beliefs. In the team approach, the answer exists somewhere in the mix of the variety of beliefs and is worked out within a solution focused conversation.

Using a Solution Focused SST to Serve Students

Most of the concerns identified in meetings may come directly from teacher referrals. In an alternative educational setting, students have the most contact time in the classroom, which means teachers tend to see more of both students' successful work and their troubling backsliding. Administrators and support personnel in a solution focused setting encourage teachers to identify anything that might appear out of the ordinary and bring it to the attention of the SST. Teachers submit a referral form to the counselor, which the counselor reviews and brings to the weekly meeting. Table 5.3 shows an example of the referral form.

TABLE 5.3 Example Referral Form

Counselor Referral Form						
Date/time request was made	*Email of the person making the request*	*Name of student*	*Student's ID number*	*Which counselor (or other professional assigned)*	*What's needed*	*Additional information*
3/30/2017	teacher@ garza.org	Kendra Williams	1234		Student seemed depressed in class	Student was falling asleep in class this morning and was seen weeping in the hall This student has a depression diagnosis
Date counselor meet with student	Time counselor meet with student	What was completed in student meeting	Follow-up meeting	Date of follow-up	SST referral	Additional information
3/30/2017	3:00 PM	Discussion of depression symptoms and academic goals	Yes	4/6/2017	Yes	Student will continue seeing the counselor until the SST meeting with the aim of stabilizing the student until the upcoming meeting where a solution can be identified.

This form also provides a method to communicate back to the referring teacher what action or proposed solution the group agreed upon and describes the next steps, including a follow-up plan. This may include a timeline for checking in with the teacher to monitor progress. Similar to any other records kept at team meetings, these forms are a potential source of unintentional harm. As a result, the forms are official documents and should be treated as such. Writing a referral out of frustration can result in unhelpful or hurtful comments, or inappropriate disclosure. Frustration may stem from passion and caring, but all staff should practice discretion when creating documentation about students and follow a strengths perspective. It is best to stay brief in descriptions and sticking with the basic facts of the situation.

Documentation and forms play an essential role, but much of the communication happening around student services is informal and based on the needs and comfort level of individual staff members. Some prefer to check in with counselors while others may want direct principal contact or feedback, still others are just fine with putting the form in a mailbox and awaiting a written response. As with any process in a solution focused environment, individualized communication fulfills an essential role. To ensure cooperation of all staff members, as well as investment in the system, the staff need to feel free to request and expect individual communication that suits personal styles of communication. This ability results from the team communicating with and getting to know one another to provide the greatest potential for effective sharing of information.

Often the procedure for submitting a new referral involves the student meeting with a counselor to provide a solution or further develop a meaningful solution. This meeting normally takes place the day following the SST meeting but must always occur before the next team meeting. For non-disciplinary issues, counselors serve as the first and preferred contact regarding student concerns or conduct issues. If counselors encounter barriers to progress, or if the issue becomes one that requires a more formalized approach, they may choose to then bring in administrative support. A counselor speaking to the student first can facilitate safer and more agreeable contact between the student and principal because the counselor can establish a safe zone for that student. No matter the context, implications of the principal's position carry significant meaning for students. By allowing the counselor to open the lines of communication in a more student-oriented setting, the student and principal will likely be able to more easily build a relationship of understanding in which the principal can make clear intentions of providing support, solutions, and answers rather than punishments.

Making Parents a Part of the Team

Approaching parents with solution focused strategies and interventions proposed by the team requires a similar process by which parents essentially develop a new understanding of the roles and motives of school personnel. By the time students enter the solution focused alternative high school, parents have likely spent a significant amount of time at school or speaking with school administrators about a child's behavior. When receiving a call or a request for a meeting, parents react in a wide variety of ways. As a result, defining specific guidelines or preparation that would suit all parent contact would be nearly impossible. Staff members at any alternative high school program are likely familiar with the fact that family structures and situations vary widely from student to student. Some parents will try anything to help their child be successful, while others may even try to inappropriately intervene on behalf of their child. Still other parents may have pulled back, feeling hopeless and thinking they have already tried it all and that something would have worked already if improvements were possible. Walking into meetings with school personnel, parents are likely to have an idea of what they will encounter and may be guarded in their interactions. Additionally, parents themselves may have had negative experiences as students in school. What most parents have experienced in the past may not prepare them for a solution focused approach.

What school personnel should keep in mind is that, like every other interaction related to the education and well-being of the students, interactions with parents are likewise about building relationships between individuals united by a common concern for the child. The parents' ideas of what could be a better outcome are potentially different from those of teachers and administrators. Meetings with parents serve primarily to establish a sense of mutual respect for one another and mutual dedication to the child. However, arriving at the point in the relationship where cooperative progress and a negotiated solution can happen requires establishing a safe space free of judgment and open to change. Changing the conversation is the first step in changing things for the student. Conversations with parents often differ from expectations staff might have in advance about these conversations. But even when the interaction is not ideal, or as productive as staff or parents might want, it has the potential to reveal dynamics that help to frame a student's experience. Even short meetings can demonstrate to parents and students the foundation for building a relationship.

For example, one student who was living with her newly born child and her adoptive parents was having difficulty at home, which was affecting her schoolwork. This is how she described how the alternative high school had affected her relationships with her parents:

> On a scale of one to ten, before attending Garza, my parents and I operated at about a 3, so pretty low. I never went to class. I did a lot of drugs. I would never come home; just rebelled against my parents. My parents would say that I needed to clean up my act and needed to go to school. I would respond by saying, 'It's my choice, not yours.' A teacher at Garza noticed my missed classes and late work, so he asked me about my home. I told him that my parents and I don't get along, that I feel unstable at home. The next week I was in the counselor's office being asked if I wanted to do a family meeting. I normally would have said no, but I trust the people at Garza. They care about me and they wouldn't invite me to do anything that would harm me. So my parents and I had a few family meetings with the counselor. We talked about communication and we shared feelings about each other. I guess we learned to tell each other how we feel and what we needed.
>
> Now my parents and I are at a 9 on the scale. I have a child. I've actually been settled down now with a guy for two years and picked up some responsibility. My parents were extremely supportive of me during my pregnancy and now I don't think it would have been so smooth if we hadn't met at Garza. My old school was a very bad school. The students were constantly yelling, screaming, fighting, beating on things. They were just all over the hallway and never in class. And the teachers were just rude and never understanding. For example, if you had a late assignment for a very good reason, like my child was sick, the teacher would say, 'Well, that's no excuse and you still get counted off.' I thought that was really rude because at Garza they have some leeway in terms of when you can turn things in, which I like better. Garza is a more laid back and easy-going kind of school and now I don't have as much anger and stress at home.

Productive parent collaborations begin with open conversation in private meetings. Even though the effort remains student centered, conversations with parents may bring up feelings that could create a hostile or difficult relational environment for a student. The private meeting provides an opportunity for the parent to shift from a position of frustration or defense, to a position of feeling like a partner who can help bring about change. The school is often able to discover what the parent is willing and able to do to support the student, which can inform the best potential solution for the situation. Often the parent has existing solutions that can be discovered through the use of solution focused techniques. The conversation aims to bring everyone involved onto the same page, which may not be agreement but rather an acknowledgment of the reality of the situation from which to develop solutions to real underlying issues. This transition creates a significantly more welcoming and safe situation for the student within an often already intimidating context. School personnel may find that a joint meeting poses a threat to the comfort of the student and the relationship between the student and the school, and may choose not to proceed in that way with that particular individual. Alternately, the parent and administrator may decide that the parent-child relationship requires unity against a common authority, and the administrator can assume the position of giving the ultimatum, thus shifting the parent into a position alongside the student. This type of strategic approach can be very useful in establishing cooperation with an adolescent who may be struggling with authority issues.

The administrator can serve as a guide for many types of parent-child dynamics. Even in cases where parents are highly engaged and well-meaning in their behaviors, a meeting with an administrator can relieve stress for the family. One student described how work at Garza relieved tension within her family:

> On a scale of one to ten, at my last school, I'd say my mom and I were at a 5. The last school didn't really agree with me and my mom is just a scholarly person. She has her PhD and my sister has gone to college. She really wanted me to do well and I had all these distractions that just didn't need to be there. She had super high expectations of me because of what she has done, but I have trouble with memory, writing, and math. We used to argue a lot. My grades, anything to do with my grades. Not turning in homework, not being there on time, and not going to every class. I thought we were too different, [but] after meeting with the vice-principal I can see how my mom and I are actually similar. For example, philosophically we are pretty much identical. We believe in pretty much the same things and have the same morality.

> Now that we have a more common ground and we see our similarities and differences, I'd say we are at an 8 on the scale. I'm also getting better grades, which helps a lot. I think we have both improved since [I started] coming to Garza.

Regardless of the outcome of that meeting, it serves as an important starting point in contextualizing what is real for that student, both in regard to challenges and potential solutions. One approach to discipline or support will not result in equally positive or negative outcomes for all students, regardless of the nature of the surface behavior. Collaboration with parents allows for a more complete view of the student's life and thus more holistic solutions.

Teamwork requires a certain amount of dedicated resources. For example, at Garza, staff members who make up the SST are mostly standard support personnel that might work at any public high school. The primary difference in this case lies in the numbers of counselors working full time in the school. While an average Texas high school may have approximately one counselor for every 500 students or more, Garza maintains a ratio of approximately one counselor for every 100 students. This ratio is a key component to a solution focused program due to the diverse and often high needs of the student body, as well as the time counselors invest in addressing those needs. Maintaining this number of counselors does require a significant commitment of resources. Due to the school's design, funds that might go to athletics and extracurricular programs at other schools can be reallocated to provide support for these positions. Support also comes from community programs that provide social workers, such as Communities In Schools, which can satisfy some of the therapeutic counseling needs of students. Outside agencies can provide a degree of assistance by helping support staff and ensuring timely and appropriate services for all students attending the school.

To ensure both the efficiency of counselor accessibility and that student needs are being met along the appropriate timeline, a solution focused high school can establish an inexpensive meeting appointment system within the school. This type of approach has been implemented at Garza. When a student feels the need to see a counselor, the individual asks a teacher to submit a request. The teacher accesses a shared online document and enters the student's name and any necessary general information which can be color-coded or marked by level of urgency. For example, a student may request a meeting before the end of the school day, or may need to meet about a schedule adjustment, which can be added to the document so that the counselor can prioritize which student to see first and which student can wait until later that day or week.

The counselors have two monitors in their offices, one of which exclusively displays this running list of requests. If counselors see that they are unable to address urgent requests on time, they can refer the situation to additional counseling staff. When emergencies do occur, teachers do not have to wait for the system to deliver the request but can call for someone from the counseling office or one of the school social workers to visit the classroom and escort the student to the necessary location. This system is meant to be responsive and to prevent students from sitting idle in the counseling office, missing work time, and waiting for a meeting that the counselor may need to postpone because an emergency has occurred. The needs of the students are central to any solution focused system, but this one is especially vital.

Counselors at Garza serve a total of approximately 350 students, but they receive around 2,000 requests for meetings per semester, which does not include the requests for services and meetings with Communities In Schools staff or college and career readiness counselors. While the investment and staff commitment is substantial, counseling services remain a fundamental component to a solution focused alternative high school and are the primary methods for reaching students who need the most help.

An Example of How an SST Works

As Ray's photo flashed up on the screen, the assistant principal explained to staff members that the student had been caught defacing school property earlier that day and that he had not been completing his homework for the past week. This was odd behavior for Ray since he had previously been attending class regularly and meeting his self-paced goals. Ray's economics teacher noticed the sudden change in behavior three days earlier and made a referral to the SST. The SST was tasked with coming up with ideas about why the young man had chosen to violate the school rules and what sorts of solutions might fit with what they understood about Ray.

After some discussion of Ray's current academic and social life, a counselor revealed that Ray's father had just moved back home after being absent for three years. Suddenly, Ray's drastic behavior change started to make sense. The team began considering what Ray's needs were and what solutions might address them. After reviewing Ray's grades and absence chart, it became clear that graduating in the spring was important to Ray.

However, if Ray continued missing class and not turning in work, his graduation date would be delayed.

Now that the team had identified the possible motivations concerning Ray's behavior and understood his goals, the team shifted focus to solutions. Rather than discussing the problem and focusing on Ray's risk factors, the team remained strengths based and talked about what Ray had done in the past to overcome academic and attendance challenges. A teacher on the team brought up that Ray had eaten lunch in his classroom last spring. During this lunchtime, Ray and a few other students were able to complete their homework early or on time. The teacher recalled Ray mentioning at the lunch group that it was difficult for him to do homework at home. Since completing homework at lunchtime was a solution that Ray had come up with in the past, the team decided to offer a before school, lunchtime, or after-school homework period to Ray.

The team also decided to keep an eye on Ray for more sudden behavioral changes. Though Ray was going through a difficult time regarding the presence of his father, the team's aim was to align themselves with Ray's goals and strengths instead of his challenges. The team noted that this was the first time Ray was referred to the SST, but the team realized that Ray could be referred to them again next week. The team concluded that this was acceptable since their purpose was to experiment with solution-oriented action; if this solution did not work, another solution existed that would.

Key Points to Keep in Mind

- A transdisciplinary approach is inherently part of a solution focused alternative school since a diversity of professional backgrounds will expand the number of possible solutions.
- To prevent problems, all staff at the school need to identify behaviors that are out of the ordinary and become emotionally supportive to students, even if the behaviors may not fall under risk factors or crisis situations.
- SSTs should include individuals with numerous specialties to ensure a wide variety of ideas to provide support and knowledge to help students are included in the conversation.
- SSTs are designed to remain individually focused. They use existing solutions and resources that the school, parents, and outside community agencies can offer.

- The team meetings remain present and future oriented. The team maintains a clear focus on the goal, even when that means stopping the conversation to repeat and remind everyone of the purpose of the meetings.
- Maintaining confidentiality, limiting the information in school records, and reducing the amount of information transferred between team members, other professionals, and parents encourage a sense of trust between everyone.
- Solution focused student services teams rely on resources for counseling and mental health services, and also work to make parents a part of the team.

Summary

This chapter illustrates how SFBT can be used within a transdisciplinary team and provides specific examples for how to create an SST to address student issues. Specific descriptions and examples of techniques for solution-building team discussions are also provided. The solution focused SST meets weekly and involves participants from many different disciplines who contribute to a solution-building conversation aimed at developing individual solutions for students who are referred for the discussion. The conversation is goal directed and present and future focused, and concludes with a specific action plan. Students referred to the SST also come to the attention of counselors, who meet with them prior to the team meeting to gather information and to develop solutions with students. The transdisciplinary team approach is essential to ensuring success within the solution focused alternative high school; all teachers are trained in the solution focused approach and work with this team.

Note

1 Cases presented in this chapter are taken from research interviews of students that attend an alternative high school and staff experiences working with these students. Names and some information have been changed to protect the confidentiality of the students involved. Some of these interviews were made possible by the generous support of the Hogg Foundation for Mental Health at The University of Texas at Austin.

References

Franklin, C., & Guz, S. (2017). Tier 1 approach. Alternative schools adopting SFBT model. In J. Kim, M. Kelly and C. Franklin (Eds.). *Solution-focused brief therapy in schools* (pp. 52–73). New York, NY: Oxford University Press.

Franklin, C., Moore, K., & Hopson, L. (2008). Effectiveness of solution-focused brief therapy in a school setting. *Children & Schools, 30*(1), 15–26. doi:10.1093/cs/30.1.15

Murphy, J. J., & Duncan, B. S. (2007). *Brief interventions for school problems* (2nd ed.). New York, NY: Guilford Publications.

Streeter, C. L., & Franklin, C. (2002). Standards for School Social Work in the 21st Century. In A. Roberts & G. Greene (Eds.). *Social workers desk reference* (pp. 882–893). New York, NY: Oxford University Press.

6 Curriculum and Instruction

A Story to Get Started

A teacher from Gonzalo Garza Independence High School[1] described her experience using Solution Focused Brief Therapy (SFBT) this way:

> Working at [a] solution focused alternative high school has brought many daily challenges and learning opportunities. The solution focused method that we employ has given me new ways of approaching the situations that arise inside, as well as outside, the classroom.
>
> One situation that comes to mind is a student for whom anxiety is a problem. She became very anxious each time a seemingly difficult concept (usually word problems), arose in her coursework. The work is not a challenge for her; coping with her anxiety is the issue. She projects the anxiety onto her work and in turn the concepts become difficult. I've watched her struggle, get angry, shut down, and go as far as threaten to drop out. I have to admit that I became frustrated with this pattern of events, at first. Then I realized that two of us being frustrated was not going to produce positive results. I know that although I cannot cure her anxiety, I can help her with coping strategies, [at least] where algebra is concerned.
>
> To figure out what methods work, I used my solution focused strategies. To begin, I picked a moment when she was calm and working. I said, 'You are working well on this concept and you seem calm. What is different today?' She told me that there weren't a lot of word

problems and that she understood the concept. To not interrupt her mood, I left her to continue working. The next time I approached her, she asked me for help with a word problem with which I could sense she was frustrated. I summoned my inner calm and began, 'You did really well with the previous problems. It is the same concept but now it is presented in words.' She gave me a look of uncertainty and said, 'I overcomplicate things and get frustrated. I just don't get it.' I took the opportunity to follow up on what she said. We talked about how she deals with stressful situations and how the outcomes have not always been favorable. I asked, 'Is there a time, when faced with a challenge, that you had a favorable outcome?' She couldn't recall a time, but she did recount situations that were made worse by her reaction to them. We discussed what was better when she did not react.

Then, we discussed the problem at hand and we talked about what helped her to tackle the problem methodically and without frustration. We used breathing techniques and slowing down her thinking. We used paper to cover up the sentences not being processed and only focused on one sentence at a time. As we read through the problem together, she wrote down information and was able to understand what she needed to evaluate the information. She executed it perfectly! Afterward, she said, 'I could tutor this stuff if I didn't overthink it and second guess myself so much.' Each time we sit together, we use the same techniques, and I had follow-up discussions [with her] about how she can transfer what she learned into other areas of her life. She has since done better and there have been far fewer outbursts and moments of [being] shutdown.

Introduction

For curriculum and instruction to be most effective in an alternative high school, the classroom structure must be flexible and small in size, with more individualization and personalization in curriculum (Alfasi, 2004; Aron, 2010; Watson, 2011). In fact, research concludes that the small size and personalization of a school community will result in higher academic achievement and are characteristics representative of an evidence-based practice. The benefits of a smaller and personalized approach can be seen in the earlier example as the teacher had time to sit and talk to the student and to personalize the math instruction to the individual in a way that would facilitate her learning. Additionally, rigor in curriculum and instruction within an alternative high school must never be compromised because to do so is a disservice to the at-risk students being educated. Unfortunately, when alternative schools do not meet academic standards, they can contribute to the achievement gap of low income, ethnic minority, and other at-risk students (Caroleo, 2014; Hahn et al., 2015). Research confirms instead that academically successful alternative schools have a challenging curriculum, mastery-based learning, and college preparation programming that rivals or surpasses other schools (Aron, 2010; Institute of Education Sciences, 2010).

In addition, research also indicates that high schools that are most effective at serving at-risk students are designed like community schools. Mental health and social services are housed at the school, and wrap-around services and various community supports are offered (Bathgate & Silva, 2010). This chapter provides examples of how to deliver curriculum and instruction in a solution focused alternative high school. We discuss an approach to curriculum and instruction that follows the tenets of SFBT and is designed to provide the following elements: high expectations and academic rigor, a goal-focused approach, small and personalized classrooms, self-paced learning, and adequate provision of specialized instructional support personnel. We also illustrate senior e-portfolios and an individual graduation ceremony, known as a "Star Walk," both of which show how the personalization and principles of SFBT are integrated into the core of the solution focused alternative school's instructional program. Finally, we conclude with several examples of how teachers use SFBT in curriculum and instruction.

Curriculum and Instruction within a Solution Focused Alternative High School

The structure and curricula of a solution focused alternative high school is designed to empower students to build their own academic solutions and to graduate with a diploma by utilizing their existing goals, strengths, resources, and motivation. The curriculum and instruction is built around the following elements:

- high expectations and academic rigor,
- a goal-focused approach,

- a small and personalized approach to learning,
- self-paced learning, and
- an adequate provision of specialized instructional support personnel.

High Expectations and Academic Rigor

Even though a solution focused alternative high school's curriculum and instruction provides teachers with a great amount of autonomy within any given course, allowing them to determine what projects and assignments to include, statewide curriculum standards are followed, and no shortcuts are taken. It contributes to the achievement gap to suggest to a student that a teacher has made the curriculum easier because the student may otherwise be incapable of understanding it. Instead, teachers in a solution focused alternative high school have high expectations, helping students identify and build on the skills they already have, so they may be academically successful. The work is rigorous and challenging, but the teachers serve as partners who are there to provide support for the student's active lead role in the learning process. Since the curriculum is based on the same approved units of study used statewide, students entering the school can open the correct file of work and pick up where they left off in the classes from their previous school.

One teacher at Garza described how she maintains high expectations and academic rigor for different students there:

> I might have some students who are very bright but not that interested in challenging themselves at the time, and I won't give them permission to read something that is below their skill level. We're not going to allow them to read Stephen King, for example. With some kids, I might give them three weeks to read a play if they are working hard and struggling with the material, and I might require another student to finish the same material faster. We look at each student's skill level and ask ourselves, 'How am I going to challenge this kid and what motivates him [or her] and keeps him [or her] going? How am I going to work with this kid who is at a different level?'

The essential point to take away from this approach is that the curriculum itself does not change. State-mandated exams must be completed and administered as directed at designated times, and students must prove comprehension of designated topics. Although these items remain inflexible, it is the environment and the way in which the curriculum is delivered that change. If a student completes the coursework for an AP precalculus class in February, she can still access a two-week review module in May to prepare herself for the exam at the same time as other high school students across the state.

Garza operates year-round, holding classes through the summer months in addition to following the traditional academic year. In order to achieve the goal of graduation, students have four periods in which they are highly focused on the core academic subjects. Table 6.1 shows a typical academic schedule used at Garza.

Garza focuses on academic curricula and the specific goals outlined within the course curricula and graduation requirements, and has eliminated sports and other extracurricular activities. Students, however, are encouraged to involve themselves in a variety of community sports that they can play across their lifetime. Even though the school does not have a sports team, they do have a mascot, the Griffith, which is a part of the school's identity. Students are able to engage with one another and socialize, but they are under no obligation to be on campus outside of normal class hours nor is there the same sense of social hierarchy, peer pressure to be a part of a team, or atmosphere of competition. In fact, one of the defining characteristics of the solution focused high school is the lack of social cliques in favor of the acceptance of everyone as being equally important and respected.

At Garza, students are never required to complete work outside of the classroom, but some students elect to complete homework in order to move more quickly through a subject. The individualized pacing schedule further facilitates a rolling admission schedule, allowing new students to be admitted and attend orientation every two weeks. The orientation and admissions process was summarized in Chapter 2. Regardless of when students enter the school, they become part of a student-centered,

TABLE 6.1 Garza Academic Schedule

Period 1:	9:00–10:10	Math
Period 2:	10:10–11:20	Science
Lunch:	11:20–12:05	Social Studies
Period 3:	12:05–1:15	English
Period 4:	1:15–2:25	Elective
Period 5:	2:25–3:35	Elective

personalized educational experience, and they never have to start over. A student might start in the middle of October, for example, having been through six weeks of Algebra II. That student does not need to start over from the first day of Algebra II nor does she need to start with the same work with which every other student taking the same course is currently engaged. That student needs to begin with the next logical step for her individual progression. Box 6.1 shows the major elements of the curriculum and instruction at Garza.

Box 6.1 Garza Curriculum and Instruction

Year-Round School

Gonzalo Garza Independence High School operates year-round, holding classes through the summer months in addition to following the traditional academic year.

Rolling Admission

New students are admitted and may attend orientation every two weeks. Regardless of when students enter the school, they become part of a student-centered, personalized educational experience, and they never have to start over. For example, a student might start in the middle of October having been through six weeks of Algebra II. That student does not need to start over from the first day of Algebra II nor does she or he need to start with the same work with which every other student taking the same course is currently engaged. That student needs to begin with the next logical step for her or his individual progression.

Multi-Credit Courses

Garza offers multi-credit courses: for example, a course that integrates government (.5 credits), court systems and practices (1.0 credit), PE outdoor adventure (.5. credits), and special topics in social studies (.5 credits) for a total of 2.5 credits. Students within this course are involved in a variety of community and enriching experiences, such as emergency preparedness, survival skills, CPR and First Aid certification, hazmat training, and criminal court proceedings.

(Continued)

(Continued)

Blended Instruction

Courses may be completed in a combination of online (using school computers) and classroom work. The technology accessible to all the alternative high school students consists of the same standard computers and software available in classrooms across the school district. The material in each online course follows the same state and district guidelines.

Online

Garza High School Online provides educational opportunities to students who attend other local public high schools so that they can produce coursework online to either recover or accelerate credits toward high school graduation. Additionally, Garza High School Online offers online review resources for state required exams. These noncredit courses provide materials for students to review in preparation for the exams.

No Homework

Students are never required to complete work outside of the classroom, but some students elect to complete homework in order to move more quickly through a subject.

Goal Focus

A solution focused conversation about curriculum and instruction may start with a problem area in the instruction of a student but quickly pivots back to the student's goal, always pointing to where the student wants to go and how the school staff can provide the tools the student needs to arrive at that destination. The following teacher discussed how the focus on a student's goal helped a student who was stuck and not making progress in her classroom:

> Initially, with my student there were a lot of excuses, a little bit of whining, and attendance issues. We looked at several different strategies for mastering the coursework that she needed. She had been in the same semester for almost a year and a half. We looked at her work portfolio and talked about assignments and work in which she had been very successful. We did a benchmark assessment to find out where there

> were gaps. Looking at the strategies that I've used, it has kind of been a mix of describing the problem/difficulty *and* developing well-formed goals. While her attendance has still been an issue, we have discussed her goals (finishing U.S. history *and* Government/Economics by the end of summer) and she is eager to meet this goal. Our conversations have resulted in finding a good fit for her with the curriculum. She prefers more traditional assignments and has difficulty with computer assignments. She is now asking questions and making progress each day she is in class. This is a huge turnaround for her.

Academic goals are organized into smaller increments that are achievable within an agreed upon time frame. Teachers at Garza often describe these goals as being reasonable deadlines to master academic material within a select timeframe. One way in which Garza sets up and evaluates progress toward goals is with a SMART goal sheet, which is used in the evaluation of student progress toward academic goals. The SMART goal sheet was introduced in Chapter 4 when we discussed goal setting. Several teachers also use a calendar to help students examine their own progress toward course credit. Both student and teacher may use the calendar to continuously assess how the student is mastering course content in relation to their graduation. Teachers use the calendar as a point of reference during solution-building conversations to help students evaluate their own progress toward their personally set goals, as can be seen from the following examples provided by two teachers.

One teacher noted the challenges of instructing high needs students:

> The worst thing I have to deal with is the lack of progress of a few students. It would be nice if I had an answer that works every time, but I do not. The thing that works the best is still giving them a calendar that lists the days until graduation and have[ing] them fill in the assignments and tests that are needed to finish the course. Telling them that they can be successful and make[ing] sure they know there is always help when they can't figure something out. Letting them know that it takes work to be successful and success does bring a lot of good benefits.

Another teacher spoke about her work with helping a student focus on progress toward his goal by using a calendar:

> I have a student, Aiden, who is not turning in his work at an acceptable pace. Before writing a referral to student services, I thought I should

> try one of the solution focused techniques that we were trained on. So, I spoke to Aiden in the hall about how things are going for him. He did not complain or say that things are bad, so I told him that I was asking him about how things are going because he is not turning in work and I was concerned. There was a heavy silence. So, I asked him what we can do to get him moving and start making some progress... more silence... I asked him when he would like to graduate from Garza. He said he hadn't thought about it. So, I got out a calendar and said 'Well, let's see where we are.' I started marking off weeks on the calendar at one assignment per week. After a little bit, he acknowledged it was indeed going to take too long [to graduate on time] at the pace he is going. But what most surprised me is that he said that he wouldn't use the computer during class anymore as it distracted him... I didn't even have to bring this up. Now that's what I call a technique that works!

A Small and Personalized Approach

Having a small class size facilitates the kind of personalized instruction that helps master the content in subject areas. At Garza class sizes range from around 12 students per class in the summer to between 15 and 20 students per class during the regular academic year. One teacher and one aid oversee each class, but the teachers, who are referred to as *facilitators*, are not posted at the front of the room, lecturing or mandating a class agenda. Instead, students sit at desks or computers, sometimes plugged into headphones, working independently, while the teacher and aid move from student to student, responding to raised hands and questions.

One teacher discussed how the smaller classroom size allowed her to personalize the curriculum to help some students progress toward a mastery of math:

> I've had some students who speak Spanish as their primary language. Since they publish the math text in both Spanish and English, I will tell them they can use the Spanish text. I will have some students who use both the Spanish and English texts, and they can take the tests in Spanish. Their grades change dramatically. I don't know if I would have discovered the language difficulties in a larger classroom. Those students would have probably stayed very quiet and would have not done well. I think we have so many students who get overlooked because we

> don't know their individual circumstances. I think every teacher goes into teaching wanting to personalize their curriculum to meet students' needs, but it becomes overwhelming when there are too many students.

Teachers are also teaching at different levels all day, working with students to individualize and personalize the curriculum to assist individuals at succeeding in different subject areas. Teachers must be flexible and familiar with the scope of their subject areas and must be able to answer a wide range of questions at any given moment.

While this may seem like a challenging way to instruct students, it is actually creative and may excite many teachers. The opportunity to work where one can use a breadth of knowledge and skills can be invigorating. This depth of teaching competency at Garza begins in the curriculum writing process, which can be completed individually or by department teams, depending on the amount of specialization needed. Just as in any traditional school, teachers share resources and teaching tools that facilitate differentiated instruction, and the special education coordinator assists teachers in modifying specific coursework as needed. The curriculum may be written to be student guided, but its tone should still invite student questions and should not suggest that students are expected to complete the work entirely on their own. When teachers are familiar with the curriculum and technically competent, they feel confident in their ability to help any student master a subject. As was discussed in Chapter 2, a specialized teacher who is an expert in curriculum and instruction can facilitate success in the writing of curriculum by being available as a resource and serving on the leadership team of a solution focused alternative high school.

Self-Paced Learning

A self-paced curriculum consists of the same goals, objectives, and knowledge as a traditional classroom curriculum. The only difference is that students can spend the time they need to develop and demonstrate an understanding of the lesson objectives. For many students at a solution focused alternative high school, the amount of individual time needed for a given lesson is far less than that required in a class of 30 students. An individual student at Garza, for example, is not asked to complete extra practice based on the needs of the rest of the class, which can result in a student becoming bored and disengaged. Nor is the student asked to move on when work is incomplete or not thoroughly comprehended. If the student is ready to move on, the individual must demonstrate that the work has been completed. Afterward, the student reviews progress with the teacher, and together, they select the next lesson or unit and set new goals. If the student needs more time or a different approach to help better understand a subject, the teacher spends more time with that student, asking questions that prompt critical thinking and helping the student to develop learning skills to identify targeted curriculum points for further exploration.

Framing the beginning of the unit is one of the essential conversations in the process of the self-paced approach. Here, teachers provide students with a starting point, working alongside them to decide on an estimated time frame for completion and providing an opportunity for student choice and preference. When an entire class must read the same book and develop a common understanding of its lessons, inevitably, some students will like or dislike the experience; some will read the text, and others will not; and some may not feel any satisfaction upon completing the coursework. However, when a teacher tells the student that the assignment will involve contrasting two novels and provides a scaffold of learning outcomes, the two can collaborate to make the work interesting and meaningful to the student while still meeting the necessary standards. A student is more likely to engage in a project involving reading *Frankenstein* alongside a *Star Wars* novel and creatively responding to assignment prompts, rather than trying to complete an assignment that insists the student read *The Scarlet Letter.* Involving the student in the design of the curriculum creates investment and interest while continuing to foster a sense of personal value and motivation within each individual.

Specialized Instructional Support Personnel

To ensure the success of all students, a solution focused alternative school is likely to employ specialized instructional support personnel. Garza employs a large number of counseling and support staff, who engage with students and closely monitor them from entrance to exit. The dropout prevention program, Communities In Schools, also operates on the campus to provide social workers and additional counseling, supplemental academic support, and grade monitoring. Furthermore, the school has engaged volunteers, mentors, and tutors from the community, as well as partnered with the University of Texas at Austin, Steve Hicks School of Social Work. Instead of requiring students to be on their own in coming up with resources that are needed to achieve their academic goals, Garza facilitates an environment where external resources are accessible at the school. The school also provides space for a counseling clinic in which social workers and other mental health professionals can hold counseling sessions and host groups, such as ones dealing with grief and stress.

The specialized instructional support staff are available to assist students who may need extra help. One example of the unique role specialized instructional support staff play was when a counselor talked about her work with a student who needed extra support toward his goal of graduation:

> In working with one of my students who is a reluctant senior, we are doing weekly check-ins and goal setting. He is also working on arriving at school on time so I am celebrating with him his curriculum advances, as well as helping him envision success with getting here on time. The latest activity [with] him [was] closing his eyes and envisioning wearing a cap and gown while I hummed the graduation song. His tardiness was cut in half and he is just two chapters away from finishing one of his most challenging classes.

Similarly, a social worker wrote about this case with a student who needed extra help to improve her attendance:

> I followed up with a female student after receiving a social services referral from the teachers concerning attendance. When meeting with this student I listened to her discuss why she has been missing school. Largely her issues were surrounding her home life and work. Her parents are deceased and she lives with another family member who uses her food stamps for himself, and she works two jobs trying to pay rent and support the three family members living in her home. Using scaling questions, I had her quantify how tired she was with respect to managing school and work. Throughout the course of a few weeks, we strategized and focused on past success to increase her level on the scaling questions. She started progressing in terms of putting her foot down at work and making herself and school a priority. The student reported she has learned lifelong lessons to apply toward relationships in terms of not having people take advantage of her trust.

Counselors, social workers, and other mental health professionals also work on the student services team with teachers to help students who are having difficulty making progress in the classroom. (The full extent of this teamwork was discussed in Chapter 5.) One teacher, who made a referral to a social worker, had this to say about her continued work with a student in her classroom:

> At the beginning of class, the student was not looking so well and mentioned wanting to work in English. We chatted a little bit and he described his mood and generally mentioned about family issues. He didn't want to see the counselor. I suggested to focus more on the reading portions of the history assignments and just jot down some notes so he can answer the questions on Monday. I contacted Communities In Schools to make a referral to the social worker. Back in the classroom, I asked him how we can improve things by one notch; he replied he wanted to just read. I mentioned it was okay to read for 20 minutes for English, then work on world history, and then finish off with class discussion on current events. I also mentioned I brought snacks (fruit) for current events. He read for English for about 15 minutes, and on his own moved onto world history. His mood improved. I checked on him and he was productive with a better mood. The social worker called and he briefly met with her. For the current events part of class, he was actively participating.

Senior E-Portfolio and "Star Walk" Graduation

All seniors at Garza produce a cumulative electronic portfolio that both reflects back on their high school work and achievements, and looks forward toward their futures and specific post-high school goals. The portfolio includes quality classwork, community service activities, college and career research, goal setting, letters of reference, a senior essay, and a professional resume. Students present their e-portfolio to family, friends, and teachers as a part of their individual graduation ceremony, the "Star Walk," which is described in the following. The senior e-portfolio can also be taken as a technology elective, as a component of speech, or for stand-alone credit. Box 6.2 shows an example of the senior essays that two students completed.

Box 6.2 Sample Senior Essay

Senior Essay A:

For a long time, all I had to get me through another day was the unreal. I would dream of a reality where I was happy. I fantasized about graduating high school and going to college. I imagined a bright future for myself. In reality, I was severely depressed; I barley went to school or got out of bed, and I didn't see a future for myself at all. I stand here today doing something that I thought was impossible just a few years ago.

My name in Mary Kate. For those of you who don't know me, you might have seen me in the library with my nose in a book, or in the art room working on a new art project. Depending on the day, I can be either extremely outgoing or extremely introverted. When I'm not at school, I'm either working or at a coffee shop drawing, writing, or reading, and almost always drinking too much coffee.

What you may not know is that I have struggled with depression as far back I could remember. In the middle of my junior year my depression reached an all-time low. My reality was warped, and I no longer saw a reason to live. I knew that I couldn't give up, and I couldn't do that to my family because I saw firsthand how huge of an effect something so permanent could be. I decided I needed a major change in my life.

I had cut ties with all the toxic people in my life and enrolled at Garza for a fresh start. I was a nobody to the majority of students at my old school, and a future dropout to nearly all the teachers there. The first time I stepped foot on Garza's campus, I was taken aback. Never before had I felt so welcomed, or comfortable in a school. For the first time ever in my life, I looked forward to going to school; however, I definitely struggled quite a bit when I first got here. I realized that no one was going to force me to do my work here, and if I didn't, I was only pushing myself back. After a LOT of procrastinating, I really started pushing myself. Granted, it took longer than I would have liked, but I'm okay with that. It gave me the time I needed to actually learn what I was studying, and to make good grades. I wouldn't be who I am today without Garza and all the amazing faculty that pushed me to do my best. I would thank each and every one of you, but we would be here all day.

(Continued)

(Continued)

Senior Essay B:

My name is Moon, I'm someone you probably know, and today, I am Garza' newest graduate. November 15, 2015 was my first day here. As well as my 15th birthday and the beginning of my sophomore year. Since day one, I've made an effort to immerse myself in this school and everything it stands for. I made friends with almost all of the Garzas staff, even if they were not, or would never be my counselor/teacher.

I've made some really special friends since I've been here and I love them all very much. I lost track of how many schools I've attend after number 25. I've lived all over the place. This is the longest I've lived in one city and school. I learned how to adapt quickly and I am very observant. I would like to say I'm easy to talk to, a great listener, trustworthy and have great confidence in myself.

I value sincerity, compassion, determination, and kindness. I try to incorporate all of these attributes in everything I do. My overall goal in life, is to live comfortably. Comfortable for me is a life of art, music, writing, creating, and activism. Contributing good to this world is what I want. I'm going to struggle, I know this, but I also know it will all be worth it.

There are many times when I thought I would never get here. As in, dead. I'm glad I'm not. Garza is the reason I'm still alive, and I mean that. If I hadn't come to Garza, if I hadn't met the amazing faculty and staff that is Garza, I would not be here today. During my time here I woke up every morning, excited to go to school. Excited to see the people that were excited to see me succeed. Garza has been my safe haven, home, and family.

I plan on saving up money for my gender reassignment surgery by working full time, afterwards I'll be saving up for my own place with very good friends for roommates. I want to go on a road trip all across the United States, backpacking through Europe, Bolivia, Japan and many other places. Sometime in the future, I'll be attending ACC while working and enjoying this new phase of my life.

I'd like to thank my former counselor Ms. Amari. If it wasn't for you, I don't think I'd even be at Garza. Meeting you my freshman year at Travis High School, was possibly the best thing that could have happened. Thank you for telling me what I needed to do before I could attend Garza, and the fastest way to get in. Thank you Garza for helping me learn to love myself, giving me all the support I needed to succeed. I am who I make myself to be. I still am learning to love myself, and that's okay.

The Star Walk is an inspiring individual graduation ceremony that is done in addition to the traditional graduation ceremony in June. Since students at Garza are self-paced, it is not uncommon for a student to graduate in the middle of a semester. Rather than waiting until the end of the spring semester to celebrate a student's success, Garza instituted the Star Walk (Franklin & Streeter, 2003; Kim, Kelly & Franklin, 2017). Participants in the student's Star Walk include the principal, the student's family and close friends, and an influential staff member chosen by the student. The ceremony happens after a student makes a formal presentation of the senior e-portfolio. The principal or another faculty member kicks off the Star Walk by stating specific strengths and qualities of the student that led to achieving graduation and the post-high school goals set. The student is then presented with a glass emblem star known as the "Garza Star" that has the Garza crest engraved on it. After the moment is captured in pictures, the student leads the group through the halls of Garza, while music plays and faculty and other students cheer, clap, and blow bubbles. Faculty members embrace the student by extending and interlocking their arms for them to pass through. African drums are played as the student proceeds from one area of the school to the next in a processional.

The Star Walk aligns with the change techniques of SFBT because this ceremony celebrates the student's ability to meet self-set goals. It highlights strengths and competence, and allows the student to receive compliments about success from the school, family, and larger community. This ceremony also ritualizes and celebrates the student's individuality and self-motivation.

How Teachers Use SFBT

There are many examples about how social workers and counselors use the change techniques of SFBT to help students, but only a few examples (e.g., Metcalf, 2003) that show how teachers can use SFBT during instruction in the classroom. As far as we know, there are no examples that actually show how teachers use SFBT with at-risk adolescents in an alternative high school and for this reason, this section provides several examples of how teachers use SFBT within their classrooms. These examples were provided by the teachers at Garza and are presented in their own written words.

Exceptions and Past Successes

Monday morning, first period. Here come the students, some laughing, others dragging in with sleep in their eyes. They gather and greet each other as they reach for the various supplies they will need to start their day in math class. They know it's time to work, but try their hardest to delay it. They sit and begin their lessons.

One student, Susie, is just staring at the algebra problem. I approach her with a good morning greeting.

She responds with a sullen tone, "I don't get this stuff."

"You don't?" [I say.] "Well, let's see what exactly it is you don't get. Tell me what you know. We all know something and from that we grow. You showed me last time how to do a problem very similar to this one. It was great. Think of what you did with that problem and how you can use that strategy for this one."

Susie stops and starts looking back at the problem, which was referenced. She begins reading over the steps and her eyes widen. Here's the a-ha moment.

"That's right!" [Susie says.] "I remember now I have to make sure to set the equation equal to zero and solve for the missing variable. I get it! Gee, I feel so dumb."

"Don't ever feel that way. You were unsure and asked for help. It's great that you recognized you needed some help and sought it. You recalled information and solved the problem yourself. All you needed was some reassurance and a guiding question. You did the rest."

In this situation, I used the student's feelings to motivate her. By this I mean she was frustrated but I lowered that feeling by reminding her of a past success. That was the 'What did you do that was successful in the past?' question. How she got there and trying that process again was my guide to help her get started. Once she realized what she did to succeed, she was not as stressed or frustrated.

Another teacher offered this example of her use of the exception question. Here is her written excerpt from a conversation she had with a student:

Teacher: "Good morning Jordan. Could I have a few minutes of your time?"

Jordan: "Sure."

Teacher: "I wonder if you've noticed your tardies? There have been 14 in the last two months. I am concerned because you're only in class around 40 minutes and I see it is affecting your progress. I do not want you to feel like this course is taking too long and become discouraged."

Jordan: [Well-known responses] "The bus is late." "My ride is late." "I have trouble getting up and parent(s) leaves early." "I don't hear the alarm." "I didn't sleep well."

Teacher: "So when you are on time, what changes occur that allow you to be on time?"

Jordan: "I get up earlier and get to the bus. It also helps that Mom makes breakfast and won't let me go back to sleep. Guess I've also gone to bed earlier too."

Teacher: "Wow, sounds like you have done some deliberate thinking about what makes a difference. So what do you recognize are some positive patterns that have helped you not to be tardy?"

Jordan: "Really I have to say Mom making breakfast gets me going and I feel better. Getting on the bus. But I know I've got to get up earlier, but it is so hard when I didn't sleep well."

Teacher: "Is it possible to set some firm deadlines to get in bed? Phone off? TV off? And see the results? Could you keep some sort of paper/pen next to [your] bed and maybe chart your results? Or can you think of some other specific options that could change your attendance?"

Jordan: "Ask Mom to buy a new alarm clock. Ask Mom to buy some breakfast that I can microwave and eat on the bus or ask Mom to leave my door open when she leaves and turn on the news. (I will have to get up—I don't like listening to news; it is very aggravating!) I can leave sticky notes for myself about time/effort. And I like your idea about charting my progress. Maybe I could better understand what is not working."

Teacher: "Wow, those are incredible ideas. When will you begin? How can I be helpful? Can I check back with you in about one to two weeks so we can revisit what is working?"

Miracle Question

"One of my pre-calculus students wanted to drop the course. She had been in Pre-Cal[culus] for three months and was making little progress, both due to the challenging curriculum and a lack of internal motivation. The only thing preventing her from dropping the class was her mom.

This student told me, 'As soon as I turn 18 in the spring, I'm going to go to minimum plan and drop Pre-Cal. That's why I don't really care about doing a lot of work in here. I like math, but I just don't know if it's worth it for me to try real hard.'

I was frustrated at her lack of progress and my lack of success in motivating her. And while I saw a problem, this student did not. She felt she already had the solution—wait a few months and then drop the class!

At last during one conversation, I asked the fantasy question (modified miracle question): 'If you could snap your fingers and make things happen exactly as you'd want them to, what would your next few months be like at Garza, and what would you do after Garza?' She said she would be motivated, work hard in her classes, and would not drop to a minimum plan. She would go to a four-year college after high school and major in engineering or biology. She admitted that she used to find math easy, but she had an awful year in Algebra 2, and now Pre-Cal seemed too challenging to finish.

With those new insights, I was able to steer this student toward recognizing the importance of completing Pre-Cal, or at least making her best effort in it, before going to study math-heavy topics in college. We revisited finding solutions to speed up her progress and give her more confidence. She came up with ideas that I had mentioned before—asking for help more frequently, improving the presentation of her work so I could follow her mathematical thinking, taking home some easy tasks like note-taking—but this time I think they have been successful because she could own the ideas as her own. In the past three weeks this student has made more progress than in the previous two months. And even though she still says she might go to the minimum plan when she turns 18, she cares enough about learning what she can while at Garza to take part in after-school tutoring with me once a week."

Focusing on Student Goals

"Since December, I have focused on keeping two specific students on a regular schedule of turning in work. Specifically, this is a focus on the 'setting goals' part of the solution focused process. The original frustration was that neither of these students was making anywhere near average progress. Student A uses her own laptop and was not always working on classwork. Student B would spend days looking like he was working, but never really got to the end of anything. What has been working for the most part is the following: the student selects his/her next assignment and looks at the requirements. I ask him/her to tell me when s/he would like his/her due date to be. We agree to a deadline and if they miss it they receive a zero or partial credit and move on. They are free to resubmit or make up any low grades from home if desired. I was amazed at how quickly they both turned around—immediately, more or less. It has made our interactions more positive. There is less passive aggressiveness from me—we have made a 'deal' and both parties honor it without it being personal. Student B has been excellent about meeting deadlines. I don't believe he's been late for any of them. Student A has turned in a few partial assignments when needed, but her grades are still excellent overall. For the most part, I feel these efforts have been very successful. Progress has at least quadrupled since December for both students."

Scaling Questions

"I try to be extra mindful when I have conversations with my students and use solution focused practices. My personal goal was to start using scaling questions. I never had trouble asking students what was different when they displayed successful behavior, but I never used scaling questions before. This, for some reason, didn't come naturally to me. After we had our staff development day dedicated to solution focused conversations, I made sure I use[d] scaling questions when trying to find a solution with one of my students. Since then I used it in several conversations; the most recent one was with Catherine, who has great grades but very slow progress in Algebra 2B. I asked her to rate her speed with which she completes assignments in Algebra 2 on the scale of 1 to 10. She estimated it at 5. Then I asked her what speed would she want to go with and the answer was 10. Then we brainstormed together all the possible ways we can make it happen. It was a very productive conversation and Catherine's progress in Algebra 2 has improved since then.

My a-ha moment was when I realized that asking scaling questions doesn't come to me naturally; I have to think it over and get prepared for the conversation with a student. It helps to write main points down and even write down the questions themselves, so that I am not 'stumbling' in the conversation with my student. I definitely need more practice and I will continue to make an effort to use scaling questions among other solution focused techniques."

Building on Competencies

An art teacher wrote up his specific experiences, provided his own explanations for what it was like to use SFBT in his work, and provided an example of how he uses SFBT to build the competencies of students as well as in student assessment:

"Garza's solution focused approach allows each facilitator (teacher) a means to help discover which students are already doing well, which might contribute to a resolution they have yet to experience. For instance, when I meet a new student for the first time, I am given the opportunity to ask solution focused questions such as the dialog below with a new student who needs another elective credit to graduate:

Student: "How long will art take? My old teacher hated my art and never let me focus on what I wanted to do."

Me: "Well, let me ask you a question. Out of all the main studio practices, drawing, painting, sculpture, ceramics…what do you want to get better at?"

Student: "I'd like to get better at drawing, because my drawings suck. They look like stick figures."

Me: "That's okay, I speak fluent stick figure!"

The solution focused approach asks lots of questions about what life might be like if the problem were solved. As the answers to these questions gradually unfold, both teacher and student begin to get a picture of where they should be heading. The clearer this becomes, the greater the possibility for true artistic expression.

Me: "So, let's focus on what you already know. What kinds of things do you draw for yourself? For fun, not for an assignment."

Student: "I try to draw faces a lot. Like I said, they are *not* very good."

Me: "Do you have any examples?"

(Student then shows me several doodles of faces in various expressions in the margins of his math notebook done with Bic ballpoint pen.)

Me: "Hey, those look way better than my stick figures ever did! Have you ever tried charcoal? You've got the basics down! A bit of charcoal could help give your faces some volume and depth."

Student: "My old teacher never let us use it. She said we were not ready."

Me: "Well, no offense to your old teacher, but I respectfully disagree. If I gave you a fresh piece of paper, and a stick of charcoal, do you think you'd like to try it?"

Student: "Sure, but won't it be messy?"

Me: "Well, it can be, but that all depends on you. Let's give it a try and find out."

I then offer a brief demonstration of adding value with charcoal using a variety of blending tools. Ten minutes later, the student presents a re-creation from the series of facial features in his notebook, now with much more volume and depth.

Me: "Wow! How did you do that? And look—no mess! I'll bet if you were to practice that a bit more, you would have a highly rendered representation of a human face in no time! So what did you think of that process?"

Student: "It was fun, but at my old school, we never did much drawing. My old teacher liked jewelry, so that's what we did."

Me: "And what did you think of jewelry?"

Student: "It looked cool, when other people did it. I tried, but it was not really my thing. I kind of had some problems with my attendance, so I never got to hear all the directions. Nothing ever got finished, and she yelled at me and my friends a lot."

Me: "Man, I'm sorry to hear that. So do you think you'd like to focus on drawing?"

Student: "I mean yeah, but I can't draw like my homeboy can. His drawings are tight!"

Me: "Well, yours are good too. You only see a difference because well, you are two different people. Drawing is simply marks on a surface. Those marks represent shapes, forms, and ideas."

Student: "So that's it? What about grades?"

Me: "Well, let me ask you a question. If you could design your own projects, what might they look like?"

Long pause.

Student: "I liked that charcoal stuff; I guess I'd like to focus on getting better at drawing people with charcoal."

Me: "Okay. Did you know figure drawing is a major component of our drawing curriculum? And it starts off with drawing facial features?"

Student: "Cool. So I kind of already started?"

Me: "Yes. Now ask me how I grade art?"

Student: "Mr. Andrews, how do you grade art?"

Me: "Suppose I give you the opportunity to grade each project you complete. Would that make a difference?"

Student: "So, can I give myself a 100?"

Me: "Yes, but the work itself should probably reflect that. So what grade do you think you'd give the drawing you just did?"

Student: "I don't know. Maybe I'd give myself maybe a 78?"

Me: "Really? That low? Let's try this... Let's walk through a typical grading rubric together."

A few minutes later, we have scored the project with a 93 and have answered a series of reflective questions to re-enforce that number.

Me: "So let's set some goals for you. First we'll discuss more about drawing faces, then work our way to more complex figures. How does that sound?"

Student: "Cool!"

These sorts of solution-building conversations have, over time, helped me find a solution for better assessing student work inspired by the 'format' utilized by the AP College Board. It's a rubric that calculates on a 1 to 6 grading scale, 1 being the lowest and 6 being the highest possible grade, similar to that which the AP readers [professional assessors of AP exams] use when reviewing a portfolio of artwork. Each rubric contains supporting solution focused questions, such as 'If you had the power to improve anything about this project, what do you think you could have done differently, and why?' Questions like this reinforce the measurable number or grade, derived from that 1 to 6 scale. With each project assigned, students complete a rubric. Upon review, if I agree with their assessment, I record that exact grade. I've been given surprisingly honest feedback ever since."

An Example of How the Curriculum and Instruction Works

As a result of poor grades, bad attendance, and intense bullying, Keira had left her previous school. Keira's learning disability made it difficult for her to keep pace in large classrooms with little support. Although Keira was capable of graduating and doing her schoolwork, she never had the specialized attention she needed to overcome academic hurdles. Additionally, Keira was a transgender woman. She started her transition at the previous school by dressing in feminine clothes and wearing makeup. When she asked to be called by her new name, many teachers and peers were confused and transphobic. As a result, Keira experienced a lot of bullying, which made learning and academic success difficult.

Keira enrolled in the solution focused high school when she was 15 and was considered to be in the ninth grade. Her academic portfolio from her past school indicated that due to poor attendance and poor grades, as she never completed her ninth-grade year. During her enrollment interview with the principal, Keira was pleasantly surprised to see her name, rather than her dead name, appear on Garza forms. The principal made Keira feel at ease and asked Keira what her concerns were about the school. Keira stated that she was concerned about bullying and keeping up academically.

"I see," [the principal], Dr. Webb said. "Those are natural concerns, but here at Garza you will not be the only queer student on campus and you will not be the only transgender student on campus. Our campus has had a long history of taking in queer students who experienced bullying at previous schools; I guarantee you will not have a problem here. The staff and students will not take issue with you being who you are. About the academics, you will take an assessment test and we will see where you are academically. Your classes will be self-paced so you will get the attention you need here at Garza."

Keira felt validated by Dr. Webb's response and took the assessment test that afternoon. After taking the assessment, teachers explained to Keira that there were some holes in her foundational knowledge, which would explain why it was so difficult for her to succeed in subjects like math and science. The following week Keira began classes. It was late June when Keira enrolled, and Garza's building was quiet and peaceful. Soon Kiera found her stride a Garza. She was addressing foundational knowledge that had been neglected and was getting individual time with teachers. Keira was meeting her goals and was receiving compliments from teachers and staff. At Garza, Keira could focus on her work because her identity as a transgender woman was respected.

Keira is now in the 11th grade working toward graduation. She often sees her peers come in for enrollment interviews with Dr. Webb and celebrates when students do their Star Walk for graduation. When Keira sees the Star Walks, she gets butterflies in her stomach. Soon it will be her turn to walk the halls at Garza.

Key Points to Keep in Mind

- Curriculum and instruction in a solution focused alternative high school is person-centered and involves a focus on student academic goals.
- Teachers are competent and well prepared in curricular areas and in SFBT.
- Teachers instruct students in small classrooms and personalize the curriculum to each student.
- Curriculum is self-paced and always meets or exceeds the state standards.
- Instruction is not about getting the student to the grade but about ensuring mastery of the learning objectives. Teachers help students learn about the academic skills they already have that they can build on to be successful in any curriculum.
- Counselors and social workers are an integral part of the instructional team.
- Solution focused work requires a greater investment in personal relationships by teachers and the use of counseling and support service resources.
- The schedule of the school is year-round and focuses students on academic subject areas.
- Admissions and graduation are revolving throughout the year, with an orientation being provided every two weeks.
- An inspiring individual graduation ceremony known as a Star Walk is provided when a student completes all required high school credits. This ceremony celebrates the student's academic achievement and post-graduation goals.
- Teachers are able to use solution focused techniques in their classrooms to help students progress academically.

Summary

This chapter provides examples of how to deliver curriculum and instruction in a solution focused alternative high school. It discusses a curriculum that follows the tenets of SFBT and is goal focused, personalized, and self-paced. This chapter then discusses the daily operations of the school, such as its schedule, multi-credit and blended courses, and the specialized instructional support personnel needed to help students achieve. The chapter also highlights how a senior e-portfolio provides an individual approach to celebrating strengths and achievement, and further shows how SFBT change principles are integrated into an individual graduation ceremony known as a Star Walk. Finally, the chapter shows how teachers use various SFBT techniques in instruction, such as building on past successes and exceptions, miracle questions, scaling questions, and building on the competencies of students.

Note

1 Cases presented in this chapter are taken from research interviews of students that attend an alternative high school and staff experiences working with these students. Names and some information have been changed to protect the confidentiality of the students involved. Some of these interviews were made possible by the generous support of the Hogg Foundation for Mental Health at The University of Texas at Austin.

References

Alfasi, M. (2004). Effects of learner-centered environment on academic competence and motivation of at-risk students. *Learning Environments Research, 7*(1), 1–22. doi:1023/B: LERI.0000022281.4968.4e

Aron, Y. (2010). *An overview of alternative education programs: A compilation of elements from the literature.* Washington, DC: Urban Institute.

Bathgate, K., & Silva, E. (2010). Joining forces: The benefits of integrating schools and community providers. *New Directions for Youth Development*, 63–73. doi:10.1002/yd.363

Caroleo, M. (2014). An examination of the risks and benefits of alternative education. *Relational Child & Youth Care Practice, 27*(1), 35–46. doi:9542835

Franklin, C., & Streeter, C. L. (2003). *Creating solution-focused accountability schools for the 21st century: A training manual for Garza high school.* Austin: The University of Texas at Austin, Hogg Foundation for Mental Health.

Hahn, R. A., Knopf, J. A., Wilson, S. J., Truman, B. I., Milstein, B., Johnson, R. L., …, Moss, R. D. (2015). Programs to increase high school completion: A community guide systematic health equity review. *American Journal of Preventive Medicine, 48*(5), 599–608. doi:10.1016/j.amepre.2014.12.005

Institute of Education Sciences. (2010). *Alternative schools and programs for public school students at risk of educational failure: 2007–08.* National Center for Education Statistics. Retrieved from: http://nces.ed.gov/pubs2010/2010026.pdf

Kim, J. S., Kelly, M., & Franklin, C. (2017). *Solution-focused brief therapy in schools: The 360-degree view of practice and research* (2nd ed.). New York, NY: Oxford University Press.

Metcalf, L. (2003). *Teaching toward solutions.* Williston, VT: Crown House Publishing.

Watson, S. (2011). Somebody's gotta fight for them: A disadvantaged and marginalized alternative school's learner-centered culture of learning. *Urban Education, 46*, 1496–1525. doi:10.1177/0042085911413148

7

Sustainability and Success Over Time

A Story to Get Started

Ms. Abadi,[1] a counselor at Gonzalo Garza Independence High School, a solution focused high school, was nervous. After taking some time off to receive treatment at an inpatient facility, a previous student had just re-enrolled in school. The student, Troy, had been suffering from substance use disorder (SUD) and anorexia nervosa, a serious and sometimes fatal eating disorder. His combination of symptoms and level of lethality resulted in his hospitalization. He had been gone for two months and, as a result of his hospitalization, had become sober and gained weight, showing that his eating disorder was under control.

Ms. Abadi was pleased to see Troy's improvements and wanted to support him on his path toward positive change when he returned to Garza. She hoped to assist Troy in preventing relapses and helping him move toward graduating. She had contacted Troy's parents to schedule a meeting with them and Troy before he began classes. In order to create a plan to best support him, Ms. Abadi needed to know how he had progressed in treatment and what was working for him to stay sober.

Ms. Abadi had been a counselor at Garza for five years and was skilled at building relationships with the students and families. Her humor, approachability, and thoughtful demeanor made students feel valued. Sustaining positive relationships with students was at the forefront of Ms. Abadi's mind. She understood that in order to ensure success with students over time, she needed to build a strong rapport with them, in part by working with their existing strengths and future behaviors. She knew it was imperative to put the past behind them and look toward the future as much as possible.

Ms. Abadi had built an especially caring and strong relationship with Troy, which made his break from school difficult for her. It was never easy for her to see students experience extreme challenges like the ones that had led to Troy's hospitalization. During the meeting with Troy and his parents, Ms. Abadi learned that Troy was to remain in half-day outpatient treatment and therefore would only be attending school in the afternoon. Additionally, Troy and his parents requested that school staff keep an eye on Troy's class attendance and behavior since prior to his hospitalization, these were signs that his substance use had increased. It was clear that Troy would continue to be a high-risk student, and Ms. Abadi saw how worried his parents were about him. After the meeting, she felt overwhelmed and saddened by Troy's ongoing challenges.

Ms. Abadi knocked on the principal's door.

"May I talk to you for a second?" she asked.

> I just met with Troy's parents and he will be at school for half days and outpatient treatment the other half. He is still in recovery, in the beginning process. I can see that this is hard for him and his parents.

As Ms. Abadi summarized the student's situation, her energy level was low. This was unusual for her since she was normally upbeat and high energy, and she knew how important it was to maintain a positive expectation for success.

The principal noticed this change. "I see," she said.

> Thank you for filling me in and doing a good job of keeping up with the student. I agree that he will need a lot of support. We will need to immediately refer him to the student services team and the social workers at Communities In Schools. We should also meet with his teachers. Why don't you make the referrals and send emails to his teachers? Copy me on those so I can be present at the meetings. Let's get a head start on his plan now and I will support your efforts. If you have any ideas or specific concerns please say so; I know that you have been working with this family for a while and are an expert on the case.

Ms. Abadi felt relieved. She needed support and validation in that moment and confidence that she was a competent and caring counselor who was able to continue supporting this student. Thankfully, the principal had an open-door policy, had built relationships with her staff, and could recognize when they needed support from her.

Introduction

Sustaining solution focused practices with at-risk students within an alternative high school means that staff will encounter crisis and stress, and often must endure setbacks to help students succeed. This is just part of the journey of working with at-risk students, and it is normal for school staff to sometimes experience disappointments, doubts about their abilities to help, and frustrations along that journey. Remaining strengths based is challenging in situations in which stress, fatigue, and even burnout may be normal reactions. The kind of emotional support and teamwork Ms. Abadi received from the principal is essential for sustaining and building success while working within an alternative high school. As discussed in Chapter 1, Solution Focused Brief Therapy (SFBT) was birthed through the collaborative efforts of a professional team of family therapists, who worked together to create a brief and effective approach to help children, adolescents, and families who experienced adverse childhood experiences and multiple problems. The importance of collaboration and teamwork has been emphasized throughout the contents of this book. Chapter 5 covered how to create a transdisciplinary team that is important to ensuring success and preventing the dropout of at-risk students. Interprofessional in composition, a transdisciplinary team openly shares knowledge and skills, and works toward the common goal of building solutions with students. The school principal and leadership team are responsible for fostering a school organization that can sustain teamwork and solution focused practices, helping everyone in the alternative high school pull together toward a united vision and a shared set of values that will ensure success.

This chapter addresses ways in which to sustain a solution focused alternative high school program over time. Research indicates that the culture of an organization can determine whether an evidence-based intervention like SFBT is likely to be used and sustained (Glisson & James, 2002; Jaskyte & Dressler, 2005). This chapter explains some crucial features of a school organization that make sustainment possible and explains how all members of the community need to embrace an official mission, a set of values, a sense of ownership of the school, and a commitment to professional development. This chapter further summarizes how to guide the school through changes in leadership, which can compromise or even destroy the school's solution focused practices if these changes are not navigated properly. Finally, the importance of continued evaluation and data collection are explained as necessary for self-reflection and continued success.

Organizational Culture that Sustains Success Over Time

For teachers and staff working directly with at-risk students, it is important that they are supported by a larger school culture. At first glance, discussions about school climate and organizational culture may not apply to direct service providers; however, a positive and functioning work environment is what allows teachers and staff to work well with students. The school's organizational culture directly affects student outcomes academically and emotionally.

For example, a school's administration has many roles, including advocating for school and staff needs, such as professional development. Drawing on reviews of the literature, Cynthia Franklin, Katherine Montgomery, Victoria Baldwin, and Linda Webb (2012) identified several attributes of organizations that have been found to be helpful when training staff in evidence-based practices. These characteristics are believed to be important to creating an organizational culture that sustains the solution focused practices within an alternative high school, and they are summarized in the following:

The presence of an organizational culture that fosters staff autonomy and proactivity, which encourages positive interactions among staff and with students. This type of organizational culture promotes self-actualization, which refers to developing one's full potential, utilizing the norms of humanism and support for one another. These characteristics were discussed in Chapter 2 as being part of a solution focused mind-set. The solution focused mind-set leads to the development of a campus community where teachers and other staff are able to be first responders during a crisis with at-risk adolescents. This type of culture is exemplified in the solution focused alternative school Garza. Garza was already involved in a mission of taking on the challenging task of educating the school district's most at-risk students. The staff were given considerable autonomy and support to come up with new and innovative interventions. In fact, the school's leadership was already exploring solution focused techniques before the solution focused consultants and trainers became involved with Garza (Kelly, Kim & Franklin, 2008).

A decentralized and collaborative management structure that promotes shared decision-making and openness to innovative ideas in day-to-day practices. SFBT utilizes collaborative and empowering relationships, and the extent to which relationships are important to ensuring the success of at-risk students was discussed in Chapter 3. Unlike a centralized management structure, which has a clear chain of command and lines of authority, and where decisions are made by management and passed down to front-line staff, a solution focused high school must maintain a collaborative decision-making process that is focused on solution-building toward graduation and preparing at-risk students for life. Early on in the development of Garza, the principal involved multiple people in the ongoing development and improvement of the school. Teachers, students, parents, community members, researchers, and even the school's data management staff were all actively engaged in a participatory approach to school governance. As the school evolved, and a positive peer culture developed, students became more and more involved in school governance.

The current principal at Garza views her staff as the experts when it comes to students. She understands and trusts that the teachers she hired are competent professionals who align with Garza's solution focused model. Therefore, when a staff member comes to her with a suggestion or a problem, she takes their feedback seriously. When an administrator does not take the needs or opinions of the staff seriously, a major organizational problem exists. Staff members who do direct service with students are the first to notice what is working and what is not. Additionally, when a staff member has an unmet need from an administrator, it affects work with the students. This type of understanding is essential to the systems perspective that also guided the origins of SFBT.

Flexibility and support for risk-taking. In crisis situations and with at-risk students like the introductory example of Troy, a solution focused alternative high school must have a great deal of flexibility, with flexible hours, many choices in learning styles, and a rigorous but innovative curriculum that is self-paced to meet the needs of its students. This type of approach to curriculum and instruction was explored in Chapter 6. At Garza, the staff are encouraged to explore new ideas in curriculum and instruction that will meet student needs. In addition, staff are supported in taking considerable risks, such as working with a student with multiple diagnoses who may still be in a treatment center, making home and jail visits to students, and conducting general community outreach to assist at-risk students. This type of work in the local community allows staff members to become advocates for students, frequently finding ways to work around inflexible school district policies that might not be helpful to the at-risk students they serve.

A teacher does not choose a high-risk student population without some emotional and intellectual interest. Taking that into consideration, the administration at Garza allows teachers to be creative with their curriculum and their classroom tools. Although all teachers have SFBT tools, the administration understands that each teacher will have a different style with and use the tools differently. There is no cookie-cutter approach to teaching students or providing them with mental health care at Garza. Such an approach would not allow the individual strengths of the staff to shine. As a result, the staff at Garza are given room for risk-taking and flexibility, allowing them, as well as their students, to thrive.

Adequate resources to carry out new and innovative practices. While money isn't the answer to every issue, the organization must have adequate resources to fulfill its mission. Solution focused high schools cannot operate on the cheap. The additional services needed to address the needs of at-risk students must be adequately funded if the school is to be successful. The founding principal at Garza clearly communicated to the school district that she would not take on the challenge of developing Garza unless the district provided the resources to create a top-notch and innovative school campus. To accept anything less than what other high schools can provide to their students perpetuates the achievement gap by not providing the resources to ensure an equal education. In the case of Garza, the school district agreed to fund a first-rate school that was grounded in the best evidence-based practices in education. The University of Texas researchers also obtained a training and research grant from the Hogg Foundation for Mental Health, which aided the school in the development of its solution focused practices.

Presence of supervision, consultation, and ongoing technical assistance that support the learning of new practices. Organizations can be viewed as learning environments. The skills and knowledge needed by staff as they pursue the organization's mission evolves and changes over time. Organizations that support their staff through high-quality supervision and ongoing technical assistance generally have more satisfied staff who feel a greater commitment to the organization's mission. Learning new practices, like SFBT, and honing those skills requires lifelong learning. Like many skills used by teachers, counselors, and social workers, SFBT skills must be continually refined and perfected. It takes practice and commitment to maintain a solution focused approach in an alternative high school. Therefore, it is crucial that the staff are provided with good supervision, individual consultation as needed, and ongoing technical assistance focused on solution focused practices.

In the beginning, Garza had the benefit of a resident solution focused coach who provided initial training in solution focused practices. As the school evolved over time, it developed its own solution focused expertise, and a more established teacher helped train and support newer teachers as they developed their own understanding of and proficiency in using solution focused practices. This built a circle of support and helped ensure adherence to solution focused practices in all aspects of the school.

The Mission and the Values

It requires the sustained commitment of an organization over time to educate at-risk students and to continue learning and practicing SFBT. To sustain this commitment, alternative high schools have to be mission-driven organizations that are guided and sustained through a set of values. Similar to a social services agency, a mission-driven alternative school evaluates its day-to-day practices through the lens of its mission, and everyone within the school embraces the values that keep the school moving in the right direction. The mission statement of Garza reflects this type of commitment and focus: "*Gonzalo Garza Independence High School shall foster a community of empowered learners in an atmosphere of mutual respect and trust where every individual is challenged to learn, grow, and accomplish goals now and in the future.*"

Along with adhering to the mission statement, as mentioned in Chapter 2 all individuals including administrators, teachers, staff, and students are expected to practice and model a core set of values that are stated in the Garza Code of Honor:

- demonstrate personal honor and integrity at all times,
- choose peace over conflict, and
- [demonstrate] respect for ourselves and others.

While this book discusses being strengths based and goal focused with students, it also asks that administrators be strengths based and goal focused with their staff. Chapter 4 in particular provides examples of how teamwork around goals, hope, and positive expectancies for success can create an organizational culture that supports positive change and promotes an environment that benefits everyone. The current principal of Garza aims to create a positive organization with stability and predictability for both the faculty and the students.

Forming a Community of Empowered Learners

As has been discussed through-out the chapters of this book, a solution focused high school is built on relationships and community, and ongoing learning supports are necessary for securing the school's identity and growth. The students are on a journey of growth and development, and so is the faculty. In order for the school to be a functioning and thriving community, everyone must feel they are growing and evolving, and must have a sense of ownership and commitment toward the school and its solution focused practices. As a counselor at Garza explained,

> You have to have a commitment first, a commitment to the school. It's not a school where you send kids for a short time, then send them back to a system that didn't work for them. It's a school unto itself. It cannot be housed in another building, not like a magnet school or anything else. Every kid on campus should be cared about, and it is part of our system. That is number one. If you're not willing to fight for your school's own p.o. box, if you're not willing to fight for your school to have its own building, its own system, then don't start a solution focused school.

How to Determine Professional Development

Chapter 2 discussed the importance of ongoing professional development and opportunities to practice SFBT. The school staff, however, benefit from other mental health training that may increase their solution focused mind-set and effectiveness with at-risk students. At a solution focused alternative high school like Garza, demographic data; graduation rates; grade point averages; attendance scores; college attendance rates; and student, faculty, and parent narratives guide the type of professional development trainings offered. The concept of a learning organization and professional development could be applied in any school. For example, if the majority of a school's staff are white, and there are non-white students at the school, professional development in the form of multicultural practice may be needed. A white female teacher noted,

> I can see that the Black males need something from me that I don't know how to give because, well, I'm a White woman and I come from a different place. I don't know how to do what I need to do, I know I'm not doing my best with them, and I want to learn more about race in the education system and why so many Black students are falling through the cracks. I'm really looking forward to the professional development the administration planned for us on this topic.

Something like multicultural practice is a skill that all school staff can build and improve. Chapter 3 discussed the importance of relationship building and how relationship building is a skill staff can learn. If teachers feel less than content with themselves in the classroom, this is an opportunity for the administration to step in with supportive strengths-based professional development. Teachers at a solution focused high school should feel excited and thrive at work, not feel afraid or disappointed in themselves. Additionally, professional development should be an opportunity for growth and creativity, not a reproachful and mandated practice.

At Garza, the leadership team utilizes the information gained from multiple sources to guide professional development and school growth. If teachers, counselors, and community agencies mention that a specific group of students are having difficulty graduating, Garza's leadership seeks out professional development to address the deficit. For example, Garza typically has a number of students who have unstable housing or are homeless. Because students who were homeless and living on the streets were being referred to Garza, the current principal worked with a youth agency and the police department to learn more about adolescents who were homeless. This responsiveness to a community need is a part of what makes a learning organization. This focus also results in more community partnerships and resources to help these students.

Through professional development, the staff learned that the population of homeless students benefit from a slower-paced curriculum, a stable school routine that includes daily check-ins with each teacher, and a focus on here-and-now goals and expectations. Since these students are oftentimes challenged by an immediate crisis, conversations that focus on here-and-now progress and small, measurable goals are extremely helpful in moving students toward graduation. Rather than focusing on the past or the long-term future, faculty take a student's progress day by day and divide the path to graduation into smaller and more immediately reachable goals. Professional development training helped get all members of the faculty on the same page. As a result, these students experience consistency in the way staff interacted with them. Clear boundaries and this sense of stability are extremely helpful to students whose lives can be chaotic and unstable outside of school. Without training to address the needs of these specific students, it would be difficult for the school to work as a community to serve them and help them achieve their academic goals.

One Garza student, Shelly, who struggled with unstable housing, noted the improved approach to teaching. Shelly said,

> The teachers honestly care about their students and there is still a small enough teacher/student ratio that you have that opportunity to be as close to the teachers as you would like to be. It's all up to you and this system doesn't work for everybody. You have to have the motivation to do things. One teacher, for example, knew stuff was not going well and I came to school crying one morning because my mom got evicted and we were living in a temporary shelter. She took the time out of class to talk with me. Another teacher, I only had her for one class, would ask me how my other classes are going or how my progress is going. She really cares that I'm moving forward with graduation. I am taking it slowly but I can see that I am making progress, every day, every week I accomplish one thing that gets me closer. It feels stable and safe to know that I'm moving forward.

How to Solve Problems and Grow Over Time

Sustaining a solution focused high school over time requires the leadership team and staff to share a vision and develop their identity. While staff and faculty educate, counsel, and serve students directly, it is the job of leadership to foster monetary resources and a reputation in the community required to sustain a school. All staff at Garza use SFBT principles to varying degrees, all with the goal of being able to assist students toward graduation. This helps solidify the vision and identity of the school. Nonetheless, it may take some time for a new program to become stable and to be recognized within the community. Garza went through a process of learning to solve campus-level problems as they arose. For example, since Garza operates all year round, and students have flexible schedules, it took some time for staff to outline the boundaries of a student's schedule.

Another common problem for a solution focused high school is being housed separately but on the same campus as another school. In these cases, there is the risk of developing an *us* versus *them* mentality, which can be distracting and potentially emotionally harmful for students already dealing with a multitude of issues keeping them from graduating. Similarly, a solution focused alternative high school that is creative and rigorous in academics aimed at graduating at-risk students and sending them to postsecondary education cannot work in conjunction with other alternative programs whose philosophy is juxtaposed to the solution focused approach. A solution focused school must be its own school with its own administration, faculty, staff, and student body all trained and taught in a solution focused mind-set in order for success to continue.

Garza learned this lesson and had to adjust quickly when it was originally housed under the same roof as the district's disciplinary center. It became counterintuitive for Garza students and staff to stay in a solution focused mind-set when they were eating lunch, sharing staff members, and walking the halls with an educational model focused on discipline rather than solutions. This detracted from the sustainment and growth of the school as a solution focused school program. Eventually, Garza was able to obtain its own building and be more successful in its goal of fully committing to a solution focused mind-set because the founding principal set a higher standard, fighting for her initial condition of having a separate building for the school. The principal's ability to set standards regarding the school's identity and resources allowed teachers and other staff to set high standards and perform their best as well.

Growth and Sustainment through Leadership Changes

Once a solution focused alternative high school is established in the community and is functioning at a high level to educate at-risk students, the leadership has to remain aware of the importance of maintaining the school through staff and leadership changes. It takes forethought and planning to weather the winds of school district policy and personnel changes, while still sustaining the school's mission, values, and solution focused practices.

Changing to a new principal can be the hardest shift to absorb and the biggest challenge to maintaining a commitment to SFBT. In the spring of 2008, after 10 years of leadership, founding Principal Victoria Baldwin retired from Garza and leadership transitioned to Dr. Linda Webb. Because Ms. Baldwin had invested a great deal of time and energy into creating the solution focused organizational culture upon which the alternative school had been built, she played an active role in recruiting, hiring, and training the new principal. Ms. Baldwin had in mind the importance of maintaining the solution focused culture of the alternative high school and knew that the new principal would need to be willing to guide a learning organization that continuously revitalized staff in sustaining solution focused practices. This meant that the principal would need to be a person who was willing to embrace continuous learning, including gaining skills in SFBT.

In describing the selection process, Ms. Baldwin said,

> Garza looks easy to the outside eye, but it's very complex. Unlike most schools where students must fit into the organization, Garza is an ever-evolving organization, which fine-tunes itself based on student needs. Garza students have not been successful with the standard school system structure, so the structure offered at Garza needed to be different. The next principal needed to have a love and respect for all students. They needed to have a strong background in curriculum and also be willing to ask themselves the question 'Why not?' when wrestling with decisions to be made. All decisions must be made with the focus of what is in the best interest of each individual student. Most of all, this person had to believe, unequivocally, that all people have strengths and it is the job of the school to help students identify their strengths. I often call the Garza students the 'walking wounded.' Garza students need to be nurtured and empowered to regain respect for themselves and the decisions they make. The solution focused model is at the core of all these attributes.
>
> (Franklin et al., 2012. p 22)

Ms. Baldwin knew that sustaining the solution focused practices across a change in principal required buy-in from the new principal, and she made it a priority to be heavily involved in not only the hiring of Dr. Linda Webb but in the transition of leadership. Although, Ms. Baldwin is retired, today she still has an ongoing relationship with Dr. Webb and the solution focused school. She is respected as the founding principal, had the school library named after her, and is still honored within the school community. Dr. Webb is an expert in SFBT, and she, along with members of her staff, leads the ongoing in-service trainings on the SFBT approach, while Ms. Baldwin and the original researchers and trainers maintain a consultation and supportive role. This type of sustainment, however, likely would not have happened without proper planning and commitment to leadership transition that made it possible to maintain the culture of the school and its solution focused practices.

Importance of Research and Evaluation

A successful alternative high school must be both data driven and relational. It is important to be guided by empirical evidence and data, such as SAT scores, grades, attendance and graduate rates, as these data-points can indicate potential areas of growth for a school organization. However, it is also important to be relational and student-centered. As mentioned in previous chapters, teachers and counselors have expert knowledge on the needs of their students. Data such as grade point averages and SAT scores alone do not represent what is occurring in an organization. It is the combination of the quantitative (grades, attendance, and graduation rates) and qualitative (staff and student feedback) that ultimately guides professional development and organization changes.

The combination of empirical data and the student-centered approach is important for two reasons: (1) to be able to self-reflect on the school's climate and use of solution focused practices and (2) to improve these practices over time. To date, five studies have been conducted on the solution focused alternative school, Gonzalo Garza Independence High School. These studies exemplify how research can help an alternative high school become more student-centered and remain successful over time. The following is a brief description of those studies and how they helped the school sustain its growth, establish a positive reputation, and evolve their solution focused practices.

The first Garza study included a sample of 85 high school students and used outcome data collected in the school setting (Franklin, Streeter, Kim & Tripodi, 2007). Rather than being conducted in a laboratory or nonrelevant setting, data was taken on the campus where the students attended classes. Additionally, the sample reflected the population of the district based on the characteristics of class, gender, race, and grade level. The study compared Garza and a traditional school on three points that reflect program success: credits earned, attendance, and graduation rates. The results of this study offered researchers and school staff insight into the potential impact of the solution focused school on these three indicators. The analysis indicated that students at Garza earned more credits than students at a traditional high school. The results of this study were important because (1) they demonstrated that solution focused schools could be as successful, or more so, than traditional schools, and (2) they acknowledged that high needs populations of students can achieve as much as students at traditional high schools. The high-risk students at Garza are not less talented or less able to attain success.

This study also examined the pace at which students' progress through Garza relative to the comparison high school setting. Findings suggested that students at Garza required more time to complete high school than those in the traditional high school. This finding supports the need for a flexible academic calendar at Garza and individual paced curriculum. The students at Garza earned as many or more credits than the students in traditional school settings, however Garza's sample started out behind and required greater flexible and more individual attention. It is important to remember that Garza students did attend a traditional high school at one time and transferred to Garza when they were unable to make progress in that setting, often because of significant barriers, such as substance use, mental health issues, and pregnancy and/or parenting responsibilities. Therefore, the results of the study indicate that Garza was successful in graduating high needs students that did not thrive in a traditional setting.

The second study explored staff and student perceptions of the school's mission and values (Streeter, Franklin, Kim & Tripodi, 2011). The purpose of this project was to help examine staff and student perceptions of the school's value and compare them to the original theory and concept of the school. Using concept mapping methodology, 14 students and 37 staff members participated in 2 brainstorming sessions where 182 unique statements were generated in response to the focus statement, "Describe the specific characteristics of the alternative school that help students achieve their educational goals." Students and staff then sorted the 182 unique statements into underlying concepts and rated them on three different 5-point rating scales: uniqueness, importance, and adherence to the solution focused model. The sorting and rating process identified 15 themes reflecting student and staff description, and understanding of the alternative school: relationships, professional environment, respect evident throughout the school, strength-based, sense of community, student-student interaction, empowering culture, cutting edge, organizational foundation, school size and structure of the school day, admission and exit, resources directed to student success, preparation for life, student success, and continuous improvement (Streeter et al., 2011). Findings from this study helped Garza's staff assess how well their current practices align with the school's solution focused approach as well help administrators identify what staff valued about the program. This information was ultimately used to create school programming to enhance what students and staff valued about Garza, with the aim of amplifying what was already working, as opposed to making drastic changes.

The third study used to guide the Garza's develop was based on student narratives (Lagana-Riordan et al., 2011). Thirty-three Garza students provided narrative statements and were asked a series of open ended questions regarding their experience in school. The students were primarily white (54.6%) or Hispanic (39.9%), and more than half were female (57.6%). The questions focused on topics related to student satisfaction with Garza compared to their previous schools, family history, and relationships with peers and family. Four overarching themes manifested from the student interviews: (1) improving maturity level and responsibility, (2) the benefit of the alternative school structure, (3) understanding about social issues and how they apply to their lives, and (4) positive teacher relationships and positive peer relationships. Students explained that the solution focused alternative high school's atmosphere was one in which teachers and peers offered understanding, support, and a greater level of individualized attention. Additionally, students described Garza's flexibility and expectations of empowering responsibility to be central to their success.

Several themes emerged regarding the students' perceptions of the challenges they faced at the traditional schools, including problems with teachers, lack of safety, overly rigid authority, inadequate school structure, and problems with peer relationships. Students expressed feelings of being judged by peers and teachers. Additionally, they felt that traditional schools were not able to offer the kinds of individualized attention or safety necessary to foster effective learning. The student narratives provided Garza's administrators and staff with insights into what was important to students and what made them enjoy learning and being at school. In order to maintain a student-centered approach, it was important that Garza's administrators did not rely solely on attendance and graduation rates as these numbers indicate *if* students are coming to school rather than what *keeps* students from coming to school.

The fourth study asked the question: *How are teachers using SFBT to engage with at-risk students who are expressing self-harming threats during class* (Szlyk, 2017). For this study, 10 teachers were interviewed individually, and four of those teachers participated in a group discussion on the topic of student mental health and self-harming behavior. These teachers described at-risk behaviors including truancy, substance abuse, suicidal ideation, and self-harm as being the most prevalent problems of their students. Teachers reported being confronted with these issues daily but also expressed a confidence and calmness in the way they interacted with the students around their emotional concerns and external threats to the student's well-being. Teachers also described building strong relationships with their students, which served as a foundation for the process of addressing both academic and emotional concerns that arise in the classroom.

Results from this study specifically demonstrated how teachers were able to focus on the academic and emotional needs of their students. This study explored how important teachers are to at-risk students and how they nurture their growth and independence over time. It also gave great insights into the types of teachers and teaching philosophies that work well with at-risk students. Additionally, it provided the administration with information on professional boundaries and the solution focused techniques teachers used with students. When teachers witness such intense challenges in the classroom frequently, it is important for the administration to know if the teachers feel confident in their abilities to teach and help students and/or if the teachers are experiencing feelings of burn out. This study was a measure of how well the administration was caring for its teachers and how well the teachers were caring for their students.

The fifth study that was used to guide Garza programing was a study to evaluate the effectiveness of Garza over the course of four years to examine on-time graduation rates and the college entrance of students (Franklin, Streeter, Belcuig, Webb & Szlyk, 2017). This study examined 1,398 students and asked the question, *Are student characteristics (risk factors, race, ethnicity and gender) playing a role in our graduation rates and college entrance?* Essentially, Garza's administration wanted to explore if all populations of students at Garza were able to succeed and if Garza was properly exercising the principles of educational equality and equity. While generally effective in graduating and enrolling students in college, one of the important findings from this study is that Garza was not as effective at graduating Latino and black males and seeing them enroll in college. While this is a common problem within high schools, this data helped the staff at Garza consider new ways to work with these students that took into consideration the oppression and discrimination they encountered within the community. For example, Latino males who are undocumented or whose parents may not have citizenship faced numerous barriers in housing and constant fears that they or their parents would be deported. These students required advice on their legal rights and what could be done to protect them while at school. Black males experienced other stresses, such as unwarranted encounters with the police and fear of expulsion, since in the past, they had often been monitored by authorities and expelled from other schools. This sometimes resulted in these students expressing a lack of trust or failing to warm-up to the teachers, or being reluctant to join in the culture of the school without additional efforts. One of the important lessons taken from this study was the need to listen to and affirm to ethnic minority students their experiences of discrimination and oppression, and to acknowledge back to the students that this is a reality in society that they must face, but at Garza, they don't need to face it alone.

It is also important for white teachers to acknowledge their own white privilege and to use SFBT to communicate to students that they are willing to treat the students as the experts about their own lives and to be willing to learn from each student what it takes to educate and help them. Teachers and other staff at Garza emphasize social justice and encourage students to be involved in community events and social activism that help counter hate and discrimination in society.

Data Collected by the School District

To sustain an alternative high school within a community it is important for the school to achieve success and for the school's staff to be recognized and rewarded for their efforts. School district and community data are important in the effort. More data showing success is better for both students and staff because data showing positive results will further increases identity and pride in the school. It is common for Garza's students and staff to be recognized at a district, state, or national level for their efforts and successes, and the school always publicizes these accomplishments. In February 2016, Garza's chess team took 1st at a regional competition with several students on the Garza team taking home individual awards. Garza received exemplary ratings in every category of the 2013–2014 Campus Community & Student Engagement Ratings. Additionally, in 2015 Dr. Linda Webb, the school's principal, received Principal of the Year from the Austin Independent School District. Furthermore, two other staff members have been recently recognized. A school counselor was recognized in 2015 by Colleges That Change Lives (CTCL) as a Counselor That Changes Lives for 2015, and a social studies teacher was featured on the district website for Garza's blended curriculum. This type of data and recognition help staff and students celebrate the school's success and aid in the sustainment of the solution focused high school.

Ways to Sustain a Solution Focused School Community

A solution focused alternative high school program sustains its success through the solution focused campus community that it creates. This community involves students, faculty, staff, school district leaders, parents, and community supporters. As has been discussed in this book, professional development and planned community events are used to continuously renew the school community and to celebrate the solution-building approach. Mix It Up Day, an event described in Chapter 2, for example, is a national movement promoted by the Teaching Tolerance organization, led students to "mix up" typical cliques that form in lunch rooms by encouraging students to "identify, question, and cross social boundaries" (Teaching Tolerance). Dr. Webb described this day as a fellowship of all people who make any contribution to the Garza process, past or present. It's a time for all people to be brought together, to respect one another as humans, as pieces of a puzzle that has created this successful and hopeful environment. Garza began to participate in this national day, naming a day in which Garza students, staff, and supporters declare there is "no room for hate" on their campus. This day brings together all the people who have made Garza's solution focused success a reality.

Eating and communing together at a hot dog luncheon brings together a myriad of mixed but kindred spirits. For example, Dr. Webb can be found in conversation over a hotdog with the beloved custodian, Leonard, and a caseworker at a homeless shelter that houses Garza students. Respected calculus teachers and Ms. Victoria Baldwin, founding principal of Garza, can be found playing games such as four-square alongside a handful of students. Conversations are held between students and Dr. Cynthia Franklin, the researcher from the University of Texas at Austin who brought the solution focused interventions to the alternative high school. Dr. Gonzalo Garza, the namesake of the school and the past superintendent of the entire district, as well as school board members all break bread together on this day of fellowship. Teachers who have been at Garza since its first days sit back and remember how they fought for the idea of creating a school to help these at-risk students, how the building was remodeled so new students' eyes turned from loss and despair to hope and confidence as they walked through the doors, and how they still return to work each day knowing they are respected and cared about as professionals. And as always in conjunction with the solution focused mind-set, the attention and respect is brought back to the students as any student who is willing performs spoken word, poetry, musical talents, or words of encouragement at an open mic performance.

Key Points to Keep in Mind

- Sustaining a solution focused high school requires a principal and a leadership team that gives immediate attention to the here and now and to finding strength-based solutions in situations where stress, fatigue, and even burnout may be normal reactions.
- The presence of an organizational culture that fosters staff autonomy and positive, proactive interactions among staff and between staff and students.
- Solution focused high schools need a decentralized management structure that encourages shared decision-making and openness to innovation.
- A solution focused high school must have flexibility and support for risk-taking.
- Sustaining a solution focused high school requires that the school has its own building and that it has distinct recognition within the community so that the mission and the values of the school can be maintained.

- Professional development is crucial to maintain staff commitment to the high school and to sustain the solution focused approach.
- Sustaining a solution focused high school over time requires that leadership and staff share a clear vision and identity as a solution focused school.
- Leadership changes require identifying candidates who understand and buy in to the mission and of the solution focused high school and its solution focused approach.
- Solution focused high schools are data driven and maintain ongoing efforts to evaluate and monitor the school's effectiveness. This data is used for reflection and to sustain its growth and practices.

Summary

This chapter addresses ways to sustain an effective solution focused alternative high school across time, explaining elements of a school organization that makes this possible. The importance of embracing a mission and set of values and the commitment to professional development and the growth of everyone within the system is also described. It further summarizes how to change leadership in a way that won't derail the school's solution focused practices. Finally, the importance of continued evaluation and data collection are explained as necessary for self-reflection and the continued success within the alternative high school. Five studies are described as examples of how the solution focused alternative high school, Gonzalo Garza Independence High School, used research to improve the school's practices.

Note

1 Cases presented in this chapter are taken from research interviews of students that attend an alternative high school and staff experiences working with these students. Names and some information have been changed to protect the confidentiality of the students involved. Some of these interviews were made possible by the generous support of the Hogg Foundation for Mental Health at The University of Texas at Austin.

References

Franklin, C., Montgomery, K., Baldwin, V., & Webb, L. (2012). Research and development of a solution-focused high school. In C. Franklin, T. Trepper, W. Gingerich, & E. McCollum (Eds.) *Solution-focused brief therapy: A handbook of evidence-based practice* (pp. 371–389). New York, NY: Oxford University Press.

Franklin, C., Streeter, C. L., Belcuig, C., Webb, L., & Szlyk, H. (2017). An evaluation of on-time graduation rates and college enrollment in a solution-focused alternative school for at-risk students. Manuscript submitted for publication.

Franklin, C, Streeter, C. L., Kim, J. S., & Tripodi, S. J. (2007). The effectiveness of a solution-focused, public alternative school for dropout prevention and retrieval. *Children and Schools, 29,* 133–144. doi:10.1093/cs/29.3.133

Glisson, C., & James, L. R. (2002). The cross-level effects of culture and climate in human services teams. *Journal of Organizational Behavior, 23,* 767–794. doi:10.1002/job.162

Jaskyte, K., & Dressler, W. W. (2005). Organizational culture and innovation in nonprofit human service organizations. *Administration in Social Work, 29,* 23–41. doi:10.1300/J147v29n02_03

Kelly, M. S., Kim. J. S., & Franklin, C. (2008). *Solution-focused brief therapy in schools: A 360-degree view of research and practice.* New York, NY: Oxford University Press.

Lagana-Riordan, C., Aguilar, J. P., Franklin, C., Streeter, C. L., Kim, J. S., Tripodi, S. J., & Hopson, L. M. (2011). At-risk students' perceptions of traditional schools and a solution-focused public alternative school. *Preventing School Failure, 55*(3), 105–114. doi:10.1080/10459880903472843

Streeter, C. L., Franklin, C., Kim, J. S., & Tripodi, S. J. (2011). Concept mapping: An approach for evaluating a public alternative school program. *Children & Schools, 33*(4), 197–214. doi:10.1093/cs/33.4.197

Szlyk, H. (2017). Fostering independence through an academic culture of social responsibility: A grounded theory for engaging at-risk students. *Learning Environments Research,* (4), 1–15. doi: 10.1007/s10984-017-9245-x

Index

NOTE: pages with a *t* can be found in tables

Made in the USA
Lexington, KY
07 August 2019